Life is a Mystery

Tom Heneghan

ISBN: 978-0-9539613-3-7

Published 2021 by: Tom Heneghan

Printed at: Heneghan Printers

Dublin

CONTENTS

WHAT'S IT ALL ABOUT

There was an ad on TV some time ago. Two men were sitting on high stools at the bar with their thoughts. One turned to the other and said: "Did you ever wonder what's it all about". The other man replied: "No". "Neither did I", said the first man. Which makes you wonder why he asked the question in the first place. Anyway back they went alone with their thoughts once more, probably thinking: 'what's it all about'.

I saw great humour in that ad, as there is in many of them. The artistic genius in some of those TV ads is amazing. Others of course could do with a bit more ingenuity. Anyway, back to our main question and I'm sure all adults have asked themselves 'what's it all about' at some stage in their lives, or have they? It's the question of all questions, and while we can figure some of it out the mystery remains.

My uncle Mick used to say that Life is a test, and who could disagree with him there. Bono sang that he 'still hadn't found what he was looking for'. The Human being is always searching and seeking for that missing 'thing'. The missing thing seems so elusive, and even when we think we have found it, it doesn't last long and the search goes on. We try lots of different things during our lifetime in our search for happiness, but in the end 'our hearts are restless until they rest in Thee O Lord'.

Some think that science discoveries prove there is no God, but might not the discoveries only prove more the existence of God. Human Beings will keep on discovering but we can only go so far, and instead of solving the mystery of Life we are just more amazed by it. Staring at the stars in wonder makes you realize how 'beyond' everything seems. Then you look in the other direction at an ant in the ground and realize she too is part of the universe. Soren Kierkegaard said: 'Life is not a problem to be solved, but a reality to be experienced.

The material things of this life that make us 'happy' only last for awhile. Then we want more and more of that material thing, but it leads nowhere. Happiness doesn't consist in getting what we want, but in wanting what we have. If we were all humble the World would be a great place. It has been said that to become humble is easy in some ways, because if we don't humble ourselves others will do the job for us. We can be easily cut down to size, but true humility is really a lovely trait.

How many Galaxies there are we may never know. On our own Galaxy we have seven other Planets beside ourselves. I always thought our homely Moon was a Planet, but it's 'just' a satellite. Our nearest Planet would be Mercury which is only 77 million kilometres away. You would have to add another 200 million kilometres for the distance to Mars. Ah, we might be better off staying at home. 'The more we know, the more we know we don't know'.

Down from above then we are living on a Ball circling the Sun. We have divided this Ball into Continents, and then Nations. Continuing our downward course we have our Counties, then Towns, Parishes, villages, into our own little gardens. Then ourselves Human Beings we go down from Adults to Teenagers, to Children, a Baby, a foetus, to an egg. Size doesn't matter! So far our thoughts can go, then we say "I don't know". Scientists will keep on discovering, but I'm sure everything will only become clear in the After-Life. Then we won't even have to ask the question: 'What's it All About'.

"Nobody told him he had to isolate"

LOOK, NO FLOWERS

There was a period of years in the 1970's when I saw no flowers. The flowers must have been there of course but where was I. Everywhere I look now-a-days I see flowers, but I did not see them for a few years in that period. Strange you may say and I agree, ah maybe it was just winter. Anyway I am writing this on the most depressing day of the year, officially January 23rd, but it feels OK today though so far.

'Where have all the flowers gone', sang Pete Seeger. Maybe the writer was in the same mood as myself. Could you imagine a world without flowers and trees. Do we pass them by without appreciating them? We have to keep moving of course, and our state is such that we don't always have the time for what we want, hopefully we need what we want. It has been said that the best things in life are free, but sometimes we prefer to spend money on the worst things. *When will we ever learn.*

Did you ever wonder if our negative thoughts make us feel unwell, or did feeling unwell cause our negative thoughts. Which came first the chicken or the egg? The older I get the more I am convinced that feeling unwell, our physical condition, came first. A healthy body goes a long way towards a healthy mind. Like everything else there are some exceptions of course. For the young maybe the negative feelings came first. Anyway, a positive negative is better than a negative positive!

Back to the flowers, and the snowdrop should give us great hope. It's the first flower to appear after the winter, even in the winter. In spite of being stuck under the hard frosty earth it manages to push it's way up and spread whiteness all around. Then comes the yellow daffodil: *Daffodils blowing in the breeze, far away from the raging seas. Then at night they all stand still, waiting for the morning chill.* Ready then for the new days fun!

'Wild flowers don't mind where they grow', went a song. I notice a red little flower year after year growing on top of a wall. I found a little tree growing on top of an old van once, it didn't mind where it grew. I took it down and planted it in the garden, now it's a tall tree. Growing anywhere can be a painful business, but the flowering at the end can be wonderful. I think I heard it said: 'we are closest to God in a garden.

On a visit to Beaumont Hospital the below poem, on a plaque in the garden, caught my attention. It was put there in memory of the young Stardust victims who lost their lives in a fire on St Valentines night. The poem was written originally for victims of war. Pete Seeger's song, 'Where have all the Flowers Gone' was written in memory of young soldiers losing their lives in foreign land wars. When will we ever learn indeed!

They shall grow not old, as we that are left grow old
Age shall not weary them, not the years condemn
At the going down of the Sun, and in the morning
We will remember them.   (Robert Laurence Binyon)

9

ADRENALINE

Lying there on the trolley waiting to be wheeled in for an operation is a strange experience. At this stage I am calm enough because all the agonising has been done beforehand; what will be will be now. It was a normal morning for the group of nurses discussing yesterday's events, they looked happy. I had to have one of my adrenal glands removed, just another ordinary days work for them

Thank God we have two adrenal glands, and they sit on top of the kidneys. They tell me the remaining gland compensates for the loss of the other, so hopefully the adrenaline will keep flowing when needed. If I am followed by a tiger I will still be able to scale a six foot wall. When Mayo win the All-Ireland there will be enough adrenaline flowing for me to float on air. I will believe 'all is well with the world', just for a little while.

Back to reality now, and I went through a difficult few weeks trying to decide if I should have this operation; or surgery as they call it now-a-days. Many a Person has gone through the same agony over the centuries with greater risk than mine. I think most people are more worried about their families than themselves should anything go wrong. Fr William Walsh's words of long ago were also invading my mind. Out of the blue for no apparent reason he said: "Follow your Doctor's advise."

I don't think we were even talking about health, or lack of it, on that occasion. Amazing! Anyway decision made, or half made, off I go to Beaumont Hospital. Mention of Beaumont and we automatically think of the hospital. In fact Beaumont is just a village on the outskirts of Dublin, integrated into the city now of course. The Hospital is situated in this village, so Beaumont automatically becomes 'Hospital'. If we heard of someone being 'above in Beaumont' we felt it was serious.

About ten of us were given light gowns to put on and get ready. Some blood was taken from me and I fainted; what a start! Anyway the friendliness of the staff carried us through to the Theatre. The Anethesist tells me that her surname is Bourke from Frenchill, Castlebar. I must find her and continue our discussion later, because she put me to sleep half-way through. I woke up four hours later minus an adrenal gland, but happy to have woken up. A man called Dr Bhro, whom I never saw, carried out the surgery; the invisible healer! (I did write to him). I suppose he can be my bhrother from now on.

I felt great that day but there was some pain later. Because of the invention of Key-Hole surgery I was home in three days. Surgery was something I thought I would never go through, but sometimes it may be the only option. The body, like life itself, is another mysterious thing. Anyway I'm sure I was carried along by the prayers of family and friends. Sr Breege Mckenna had given me a miraculous medal and said: 'God Bless the Doctor', and so say all of us in times like this.

Adrenaline is a funny thing
It lifts you in the air
But sometimes when you need it
It isn't always there

It doesn't take the lead
It reacts to circumstance
It makes you feel uplifted
In rare moments of chance

Too much of one good thing
Is not good for anything
So rest awhile adrenaline
Until my lonely heart will sing

Adrenaline is flowing here

TO BEE A WASP

I never thought I would find myself missing a swarm of wasps. They had encamped in the shed right outside our back door. They found, or made, a little hole in the wall where they buzzed in and out. We had to proceed with caution every time we went outside. They had built their home on the ceiling of the shed and their art-work was amazing; a round dwelling the size of a football.

"What do I do now", I wondered, as they could be dangerous if the wrong move was made. "You can either spray them, or let them die naturally in November", I was told. I did not like to kill them so I took a risk and waited until they disappeared in November. I watched them going and coming every day from my window. This was definitely a 'Meitheal' (working-group) in the best sense of the word. Actually bees decide as a group where to build their hive, thousands of them, not the queen bee.

One day I noticed a little black bee creeping slowly towards the hive. I wondered what would be the reaction of the wasps towards a little bee. They kept buzzing in and out and seemed to ignore him, but I just hope he got a good reception inside. Actually I thought it was only bees that made honey but wasps do too it seems. When I was young I only saw an odd wasp, but plenty of those homely black bumble bees.

Now it seems to me there are many wasps and very few humble bumble bees. Since I started writing I heard that its's only Mexican wasps that make honey. Do we have Mexican wasps in Ireland, or are my wasps bees. Anyway I believe the bees are dwindling and that's bad for all of us. "If bees disappeared from the face of the earth Humans would last no more than four years," so said Albert Einstein. It sounds dramatic so we must look after the bee family, it's to bee or not to be!

St Molaga is the Saint of bees. He was born in Timoleague, Co Cork and became a bee-keeper in Wales. On his return to Ireland some bees clung to him. He must have treated them gently. He set up a Church at Braemore, Balbriggan, beside which stands the local St Molaga Primary School today. I don't want to confuse the issue here but St Gobneit is actually the 'Patron' saint of bees. The more help the bees get the better, so two saints are better than one.

Anyway, back to my own colony and as November comes our wasp family begin to dwindle. Their lifetime, a few months, was over and I thought how sad it was. One humorous wasp started singing: 'what will bee will be'. I was told that the queen wasp would live on and build again the following year. A year passes and guess what, the wasps are back closer than ever. Now they buzz in and out at the back door-step, living right under the kitchen floor.

Lots of honey down there I would imagine, but I won't be taking it off them. I believe it's for themselves they make the honey anyway, so enjoy. I actually thought they made it for us humans, so maybe we should be making our own honey in whatever form. While the wasps die the queen lives on I believe. I don't know how long she lives, but I hope she emigrates next year. A Queen she may be but I should be King of my own castle. In the meantime all I can say to my under-ground neighbours is: "Bee-hive yourselves wasps."

Happy to be a busy bee, or even to be a wasp
Flying in and out all day, with nectar in my grasp
I pollinate the flowers, roses of every hue
Happy to see me coming, after the morning dew

I have a busy wasps life, but I keep on buzzing
Humble bumble black bees, I hear them humming
Humans use our honey, amazed what we can make
Each to one's own duty, for one another's sake

Out I fly each minute, another flying in
We keep the honey flowing, in the noisy din
Back again to home-land, under the kitchen floor
I use the lowly entrance, Humans use the door

THE SOUND OF MUSIC

Music comes in all types of sound now-a-days. At my age classical seems to be taking me over and can put me into a state of ecstasy; but you don't stay there long in this life. I do like Country and Western too as there's a certain nostalgia in those songs which makes you feel sad and happy at the same time. There are certain songs which stop you in your tracks when heard out of the blue on radio. Evoking memories of a certain time and place.

I went to see 'The Sound of Music' film in 1967, and what a nice experience that was. I had no idea what it was all about going in, but I came out uplifted. It is based on a true story, and the film was shot where the story took place: Salzburg amongst the beautiful mountains of Austria! The songs were written by the men of the Musicals 'Rogers and Hammerstein', and the film was produced and directed by Robert Wyse.

I was just thinking recently about the importance of music in films. Apart altogether from musicals every film depends enormously on music. We don't think about the music but it's always there in the background, and the success of any film often depends on the right music. It's only when the music stops occasionally we realise there was music. There is a song called 'The Sound of Silence', and you can hear silence too when the music stops for awhile. 'Silence is Golden' went another song of my younger days.

'The Sound of Music' originated from the autobiography of the real-life Maria Von Trapp. She wanted to be a Nun but the Reverend Mother had her doubts. Maria loved music and ended up looking after seven children, and teaching them 'music of course'. What wonderful performances from the two main actors, Julie Andrews as Maria, and Christopher Plummer as the Captain. The children's voices amongst the edelweiss flowers cap the film. Sadly two of the Children, Liesel and Louisa, have passed away recently as I write.

Rodgers and Hammerstein have written other musicals, like 'Oklahoma' for example and Carosel which has the often-sung 'You'll Never Walk Alone' in it. That song was later recorded by Liverpool band 'Gerry and the Pacemakers', and has become the anthem of Liverpool football followers at Anfield and beyond. 'The Sound of Music' was the Duo's last musical as Hammerstein died in 1960 shortly after the premier of the stage production. He never saw the Film, but it's nice to leave something after us when we go.

Edelweiss, maybe snowdrop for us, is a cute little song, but the most beautiful and meaningful of this film songs is 'Climb every Mountain'. *Climb every mountain ford every stream, follow every by-way till you find your dream. A dream that will ask all the love you can give, every day of your life for as long as you live'.* Every day of our lives for as long as we live, ooh! We forget that sometimes, and think we can opt out now and again, but it's every day!

Ah, just heard that the Captain, Christopher Plummer, has passed away. God rest him! Like a lot of things in life we take music for granted, and there is so much of it now. When we only had the old Gramaphone, and then the Radio, we appreciated music and song more I feel. As the old saying goes; 'Too much of one thing is no good for nothing'. Anyway, every generation comes up with its own master-piece in music. Creative minds there will always be. We certainly need silence in this noisy world of ours as well, but the sound of music often gives us a lift when we are low.

Tubberclair is *alive* with the sound of its *choir*

BEETHOVEN 250

Let's go back in time now, back to the great composers. This year is the 250th anniversary of the birth of Beethoven. He was born in Bonn, Germany in 1770, and later he was to drop out of school to support his family. Unlike others before him he translated feeling into music. He gradually became deaf but amazingly he composed his greatest piece in 1824 when totally deaf, that being his 9th symphony. Just three years later he has passed away in Vienna, the great classical city.

The period of the great classical composers seems to be the 18th and 19th century, although Stravinsky did not die until 1971. Many of them have lived around the Central Europe area. While they were great composers that did not always translate into money. Many of them struggled financially and seem to have suffered more than their share of life's misfortune and frustration. It was as if they composed their great compositions in this life, but had to wait for their reward in the next.

Schubert said: "It sometimes seems to me as if I did not belong to this world at all". He wrote hundreds of beautiful songs, but many were not appreciated until after his death. He wrote one of the most beautiful of the 19th century on the back of a menu in a dim-lit café. His famous 'Unfinished Symphony' was not recorded until 1865, 37 years after his death. He was only 31 when he passed away, Beethoven being his musical hero.

Two other famous composers died also in their 30's: Mozart and Mendelssohn. Most of the great Composers had great faith and attributed their music to a gift from God. Haydn in particular never stopped thanking God and, unlike some others, he was recognised as successful and joyful in his own lifetime. He said: "Since God has given me a cheerful heart, he will forgive me for serving him cheerfully". Mendelssohn could be said to have a similar disposition ass Haydn.

'Handle with care!' Handel was German but lived most of his life in England. He also suffered his fair share of rejection, and in fact was about to give-up when a commission for him came from Dublin, to compose something to raise funds for a charity. In 24 days he had composed the Messiah, with it's famous Halleluia Chorus. It was premiered in Dublin in 1742 as a Charitable benefit concert, and raised 400 pounds, freeing 140 men from debtors prison. That was the start of many other benefit performances from Handel and the Messiah.

Our great Irish composer Sean O'Riada was another to die at a young age, he being just 40. It's amazing what you can achieve in a short life too. It's like as if O'Riada dug up from the earth the music tradition that was buried there for centuries. Lovely rugged sound! I wondered why all those great composers seemed to come together at a certain period in time. It may be of course that we have great composers amongst us now too who might be discovered later, even after death. However, it would be hard to match the great composers like Beethoven.

HINDSIGHT

Isn't it amazing how clear things become just after you have done something, or said something, 'the wrong way'. "Why didn't I think of that", we say. You can spend days thinking things over about a decision to be made, and still it's often only clear after the act. It's like as if our minds are muddled until we act, and then everything is as clear as daylight. We seem to put the cart before the horse sometimes.

Former Taoiseach, Bertie Ahern, once said: "If hindsight were foresight I'd be a millionaire". Interesting and amusing words, and it's hard to argue against them. Now, we are of course Human Beings so we can't expect everything to be clear. Otherwise we wouldn't have much of a challenge in Life. 'Who said we want a challenge', you might ask. Some are up for a challenge, others can do without it.

'Regrets, I've had a few' went the song; didn't we all. That again is part of the human condition, so there's no point in dwelling too long on them. More to come maybe! Luckily for us we have made more than one mistake. If we only made one mistake we would be regretting it all our life saying: "How did I let that happen?". When we make quite a few mistakes we say: "Well, that's the way life is", and we move on. 'It is what it is', as some say nowadays, meaning 'things are the way they are'. Even if we would like them to be different we accept our fate.

Regretably too we sometimes make the same mistake again and wonder why. We should have learned from past mistakes, but here we are again with the same one, and that's another regret. Regrets can be like resentments, except regrets are against ourselves. Resentments are against others, or so we think. It has been said that 'resentments are like taking poison and hoping the other person will die'.

Hindsight may not be all it's cracked up to be either. What we think is a bad decision in hindsight, may sometimes turn out differently with the passage of time. Other factors come into play that we hadn't foreseen in hindsight. There is a hindsight to hindsight, if that's not a contradiction. Hindsight should help us focus better for future decisions though. We need to 'look before we leap' unless we are procrastinator's. On rare occasions we may need to 'leap before we look'. We have to take a risk at times, otherwise we get stuck and can't move on.

The decisions we make in life depend of course on a lot of things. Our health, our confidence, our circumstances all help our decision making. Two people can make totally opposite decisions to the same situation, and both can be right. So now, not only have I given you hindsight but also the hindsight of hindsight. However, while we could get stuck in a groove with too much procrastination, thought-full foresight may be the best after all. I'll finish with a joke of mine: 'The best way to get rid of procrastination is to keep putting it off". Let's stay focussed now.

If hindsight were foresight how would we be
No decision to make, would we then be free
No egg on our face from now-made decision
It's goodbye to hindsight no more derision

Foresight would make hindsight disappear
We'd look into the future like any good seer
No frustrated thinking of what should I do
This action of mine no more would we rue

Hold on a minute, all bored we might be
No challenge to meet, no one to disagree
Exercise no more for my formidable brain
I'll hold on to hindsight, I'll be more sane.

Foresight: "wait for my *signal*"

WE'LL SEE

Sometimes when children ask for something the Parents answer: 'we'll see'. It gives the Parents time to think things over and it satisfies the child for now. The 'we'll see' in this case of course is seeing with the 'minds eye'. Anyway, did you ever wonder what blind people see in the minds eye. I decided to check this out with a man who lives beside me here in Balbriggan. Tom O'Neill of the Ballindine clan.

I pay an odd visit to Tom in his cosy home in the company of his Guide-Dog Qeb, but the dog makes no comment, just an odd glance! Tom is still in mourning as his wife Breege has just passed away, and he has great memories of her. He calls her his life-time friend! She spent three months in the eye and ear hospital when she was a baby with no visits allowed. After that she had a lifetime of visiting doctors and clinics, and many operations for her sight.

Tom and Breege's sight disability did not stop them from helping others. They both got jobs in the Civil Service with revenue and fought for the rights of others with disability, which in turn got Breege promoted. Tom's job, amongst others, brought him around the Country giving talks. Being people of such initiative 'Irish Guide Dogs for the Blind' was an obvious choice of 'Association' for them, and they set up a branch in Balbriggan in 1987.

Tom also visits schools and he was impressed when a child asked him if he dreams. He said 'yes', as he didn't start losing his sight until he was 20. So it's interesting that he can 'see' in dreams. I met another inspiring girl, Audrey, who is blind from birth and she dreams in 'feeling' rather than seeing anything. For example if she dreamed she was on a train journey she would feel the rocking. Many a train journey Tom and Breege took, assisted by Kevin at Heuston Station. The couple had wonderful helpers in their lives and in all their initiatives.

We don't always appreciate what we have, dwelling instead on what's missing. It's amazing what we can achieve when we put our minds to it. We all have an 'achilles heel' whether it be physical or mental. Sight or no sight we all grope in darkness at times, but if we make good use of what we have we often forget about what we don't have. While Tom has no sight I'm sure he has gained good insight. The insight I gained is that blindness is what it is; a dark world physically. But my meeting with Tom made me 'see' 'life is what you make it'.

Andrea Boccelli is blind and has probably the most beautiful singing voice in the world. His blindness did not stop him using it. The Jewish Talmud says: *'We see things not as they are, but as we are'* Tom was Leader of the North Co Dublin Guide Dogs Association for many years. He has just retired from that job now, but no doubt he is still working behind the scene. He said he got his first Guide Dog in 1985, and it transformed him.

Tom and Breege had just celebrated their Ruby wedding anniversary when Breege passed away. They visited many places with their humble Guides. You might be thinking they visited their original homes in Ballinalea, Longford and Ballindine, Mayo. They did, but wait for it, they went on a cruise from San Francisco to Mexico for their 25th wedding anniversary. They also made history as their's was the first guide dog to travel in an aircraft cabin across the Atlantic. Then for their 30th anniversary they went to Capetown in South Africa, and visited the cell of Nelson Mandella. These are journeys, with my sight, I would hesitate to make. While seeing is believing, believing is also seeing in a sense.

Breege, Tom and transformer Gatsby

CONNEMARA INTERNATIONAL

Connemara is as Irish as you can get. When you are here you can say: 'this is Ireland'. Rugged is the best word to describe this place. Mountains and more mountains are the feature here. And of course we have the Atlantic Ocean lapping the shore. It's from the sea actually that Connemara got it's name, meaning: descendants of 'Con Mhac of the Sea'. It's unusual to have such a large tract of land under one name. The Burren in Clare might be similar in that regard.

Connemara is in Co Galway and it's impossible to stop it crossing the border into Co Mayo in places. The road from Leenane to Louisburg is breadth-taking in its beauty, and has the counties borderline somewhere along the way. This road area has a certain tranquility about it with mountains on either side. The streams, little lakes and waterfalls soothe the mind. Hopefully it drowns out our negative thoughts for awhile.

International then would seem the last word you would think of for Connemara. However, the mountains give us the beautiful green Connemara Marble. This marble has been used in The Cathedral in Galway, in Westminster Cathedral and the Senate Chamber in Pennsylvania. The beautiful Kylemore Abbey, cosy amongst trees and mountain, draws many International tourists and the Irish too of course.

The First ever Translantic flight to Europe landed in Connemara, just 100 years ago; at Derrigimlagh to be precise. This feat was achieved in 1919 by two British men John Alcock and Arthur Brown. It was a landing without a runway, what's a runway! At least the landing site looked nice and flat, but they did not realize it was a bog, so it might have been soft but bumpy. It's amazing what some people have ventured, with no help from the ground then. They probably never heard of a place called Connemara before that, but never forgot it afterwards.

They landed beside the Marconi Wireless Station, and that's another Internationl dimension to Connemara. It also turned out to be a good landmark for the two flight pioneers. .John Alcock died six months later in a plane crash in France. It was probably a less dangerous flight than the translantic one. He had done the hard part and survived, only to die in less dangerous circumstances; such is life.

The 'The Quiet Man' film, starring John Wayne and Maureen O'Hara, was shot in Connemara. This film showed Connemara in all its beautiful rugged scenery to the world. I suppose Connemara Ponies also have an International dimension, and the Currachs at Sea are there for international tourists to view. If we go further afield, or a-sea, a few miles out from the coast we have the famous Aran Islands. What stands out here are the stone-walls, fencing fields and tiny roads.

Back to Connemara, with no stone walls, but plenty of rocky land. It's often windy here and there are not many trees to block this wind, but if there were it might not be Connemara. After a day negotiating the mountains you can relax in the tranquil town of Clifden. Connemara is an Irish speaking area, imagine speaking Irish in Ireland, but like all places of the World English has seeped in. There are other interesting places in Ireland of course, but this place is unique. That's Connemara in a nutshell, where international tourists flock in, and if you want to crack the shell come and see it for yourself.S

Back to their roots from Foreign Shores

FR TOM ON BRIXTON HILL

There were two Tommy Heneghan's living within a mile of each other. One of them was me, of which we will say no more here. The other was Fr Tom. He was born on the 11th November 1949, and grew up on Castleucas Hill, Ballyglass, Co Mayo. At the bottom of the hill stands the Grotto of Our Lady. He had a clear view of Croagh Patrick to the west, Neiphin to the north, and many other places in between on a sunny day.

Tommy was ordained to the Priesthood in 1973. There are many people in Society doing the corporal works of mercy, but we need people also doing the spiritual works. 'Man shall not live on bread alone!' Although you could say both works often merge into each other. Anyway if you are called in one direction, Go! Interestingly enough, for such a small place, another Castlelucas man went as well. He being Fr Anthony Joyce who served, amongst other places, in Balbriggan from 1931 to 1938.

The now Fr Tom for most of his life after ordination ministered in different Parishes throughout southern England. There was one exception when he spent a six year stint in Ecquador, a long way from home. That was a great experience for his future pastoral work and his final move to Brixton Hill London, a far cry from his Castlelucas Hill. Corpus Christi Parish on Brixton Hill is one of the most diverse Parishes in Britain. He ministered there tirelessly serving poor and rich alike.

He brought people together with his gentle ways and wisdom. In the midst of all his work he was to pass away suddenly with a heart attack on the 6th March 2013, at the relatively young age of 63. A great loss to his Parish and Family! A Brixton Councillor Rachael Haywood commented: "Fr Tom was a gentle, extraordinary rare man who radiated goodness and humanity". Another Parishioner commented: "So sadly missed Fr Tom from our Parish, and you made any Mass a pleasure to be in. I could listen to your voice and accent all day". Yes, that Castlelucas accent can be captivating.

Speaking of the Mass reminds me of a young Italian Teenager who was recently Beatified, next step to Sainthood. He was a modern computer whizzkid who died at the age of 15 of leukaemia in 2006. Carlo Acutis used his IT skills to program web-sites documenting Eucharistic miracles. Now how rare is that in Teenagers, very I would say, but maybe less than we think. Carlo said: "Everyone is born an original, but many die like photocopies".

Back to Fr Tom and many Eucharists he has celebrated for his people. The Castlelucas accent will be missed on Brixton Hill, but not forgotten. I should have kept in touch with my name-sake, but how often do we say that! In fact when he passed away some people thought it was me, but I had to tell them that 'news of my passing was greatly exaggerated', as Mark Twain once said. Anyway, that's Tommy Heneghan from Castlelucas in the smallest nutshell you could find. God rest him.

THE OLD BOG ROAD

'But here was I on Broadway, a-building bricks per load. As they carried out her coffin, down the old bog road'. It's interesting that the words of this beautiful sad song were written by a Lady (*Teresa Brayton*). She had to get inside the head of Paddy working on the buildings in New York, as his Mother was laid to rest at home. *'There were snowdrops and primroses piled high above her bed, and Ferns Church was crowded as the funeral Mass was said'.*

Emigration has provided us with many beautiful, but sad, songs. Perhaps 'The old Bog Road' is the saddest of all. 'I'll Take You Home Again Kathleen', and 'Galway Bay' can rival it for sadness I suppose. Maybe the most beautiful songs are written in sadness, as there is a greater depth to them. Did I read somewhere that 'I'll Take You Home Again Kathleen' is not an Irish song at all? So other countries no doubt had their own sad songs to write.

One day Paddy lay down his slan, turf spade, and headed for far-off America. After the famine of 1847 many an Irish person, even Families, made that same journey. They didn't know if they would arrive never mind what lay ahead of them in the New World. Some held American wakes, meaning often no return. How did they do it we wonder, but some did go on to become successful beyond what they thought possible.

I took a drive down that 'Old Bog Road', and the hawthorn trees are there shading the road, and renewing the memories. It's surprising not to see a restaurant there called, obviously, 'The Old Bog Road'. Our Ancestors built the sky-scrapers and railways, in far-off Lands, with blisters on their hands: *My weary hands are blistered through work in cold and heat. And oh to swing a scythe again through a field of Irish wheat'.*

The grandchildren of our Ancestors, who never returned, are now returning to find their roots. It's an emotional journey as they can see in their mind eye Paddy laying down his slan, and heading across the Atlantic. I had a go at the slan myself in Kilboyne bog, but mostly it was the spreading of the turf. I believe they are not putting chimneys on new houses anymore, no more the sight of gentle rising smoke in the evening sunset. As I write the 'Peat Briquette' is also coming to an end. You could have called it the 'Fillet of Turf'

Teresa Boylan, Brayton being her married name, was born in Kilbrook, Kilcock, Co Kildare in 1868; near the old bog road. She spent many years in America herself, so you can feel the home-sickness in her song as she wrote the words. Madeline King O'Farrelly from Rochfordbridge, Co Westmeath put music to the lyrics. She certainly got a feel for 'The Old Bog Road' with that haunting air. Now that turf is finally disappearing the old bog road will be older still, but at least the walking tourists will have the memories.

Most Irish homes had their own bog road to travel, and the memories of those days the young will never have. "Dad, what's a bog"? "A Bog, oh it was a unique place of Irish activity, now it's a place of Irish history" The Young will have their own memories of course far removed from the old bog road. I suppose it's more a time for thinking heads now than for moving bodies. The old generations had their physical exercise in their work, two in one! Henry Ford once said: "Cut your own wood, it will warm you twice". *'God be with you Ireland, and the Old Bog Road'.*

"Master, I miss the bog"

THE HAT FACTORY

I had been wearing a peaked cap for some time when one day I turned it over to see where it was made. To my surprise it said 'Made in Castlebar'. I attended school right beside the Hat Factory but being young I took no notice of it. Many a farmer wore a peaked cap, but I never knew they were made in the hat factory. Then again they would hardly be made in a jam factory. The peaked cap is still going strong today.

It's not every town that has a Hat Factory so it was nice to 'discover' it, even though it's now gone. The actual building is still there I believe though. Anyway I decided to look into a little bit of the history of this unique industry. The Hat Factory was built in 1939, and it was run on steam power. There were natural resources of turf and water nearby. Kilboyne bog comes to mind, and Lough Lannagh was just lapping at the back door.

It was the first factory of its kind, west of the Shannon, to use natural resources. Up to 300 People were employed here at one stage, one of the largest employers in the region. A siren went off to call People to work. In the early morn the hat factory horn brought people from Islandeady, Snugboro, Turlough, Breaffy, Frenchill, Ballyheane, and the Town of course. It had a 300 foot high chimney which became a landmark for the surrounding area. There were also underground passages.

This Factory had an international dimension to it from the off. It was built by Checho-Slovakin refugees who were fleeing from the 2nd World war. I didn't know we had Refugess in Ireland at that time. The Architect was Belgian Auguste Koettegen, and the Manager was Franz Schmolka from Prague. Let's not forget the locals without whom the Factory would not have got off the ground. The contractors being J. P.McCormack and James Chambers.

Who would ever have thought of building a Hat Factory, above all things, in Castlebar at that time? George Bernard Shaw's saying comes to mind: *"Some People see things as they are and ask why? I dream things that never were and ask why not?"* Well the idea came to local Castlebar business-men who were looking around for an Industry for the town. People like J.E. McEllin who also became a director at the Factory. A Hat Industry in Belgium came to their attention, so they pursued that avenue. Some staff from the Castlebar Plant were sent to Belgium to learn the trade.

Those Business-men overcame many obstacles, including lack of materials because of the war, but stuck to their task. The dream became reality, and the Hat Factory was born, opening its doors in 1941. The humming machines blending with the humming of the workers created a nice atmosphere in the Town for 40 years. In the midst of a w orld war the locals made hats! A great achievement, so Hats off to all involved in the setting-up and running of Castlebar Hat Factory.

MODERN MEANS

The modern generation have laptops, iphones, smart-phones, ipads, etc, and new things cancelling each other out. I have got as far as emails, but I seem to be way behind in the fast moving 'modern means' stakes. The modern way of communicating is instant, far removed from the telegram and letter. The telephone was a great invention for its time though. That was way back in 1876, by A. Graham Bell. Elisha Gray invented a telephone also at the same time. You wait thousands of years for a telephone and two come along at the same time!

I remember travelling through the little hills of Ballyshaun, Breaffy and arriving at my Uncle Pat's house. There we found this amazing instrument called a Radio, and voices coming out of it. The World must be coming to an end we thought, but it didn't stop us from listening to Micháel O'Hehir, telling us about a match in a far-off land called Dublin.

I met the other Micháel (O'Muirchetáigh) recently and he told me that the first radio broadcast of a GAA match was back in the 1920's. Actually the first live broadcast of a field sports game, outside the US, was for a hurling game. It was an All-Ireland semi-final between Kilkenny and Galway, and took place on the 29th August 1926. This match was broadcast by P.D.Mehigan on Ireland's first radio station 2RN. It may have paved the way for 'Match of the Day'.

Recently I discovered an old copy of 'Jimin' in the attic. It revived memories of our struggle with Irish in primary school. It was a hard slog then, so I am now reading it again after all those years. I heard somebody recently saying that we Irish People have a sleeping giant of the Irish language inside us which needs to be re-awakened. It was words to that effect anyway, and I thought it a very enlightened statement. Some day soon this giant will roar again perhaps. Maybe when we have a united Ireland

As long as we have Micháel O'Muirchetáigh we will always have the sound of *'Irish'* resounding in our minds. He said on one broadcast: "He has the ball, he's going through, he's in front of the post's, he takes his shot, and the ball is in the Nally Stand". Meaning he sent it a mile wide. He has humour and friendliness in his voice. He's part of what Ireland is, or should be. That Nally Stand is no longer in Croke Park, but I think it still 'stands', in Tyrone now. It is named after Balla, Mayo Athlete Pat Nally. He encouraged Michael Cusack with the founding of the GAA in 1884.

So what other inventions are to come which will amaze us. Nothing will amaze us any more I imagine. The next thing might be travel by thought. We say; "I need to be in Dublin now", and we will arrive there just by thought process. No traffic jams, but thought jams perhaps. It may not happen, but if it did it would not amaze us at this stage. Of course with modern means we don't need to go anywhere, everything comes to us. Anyway, Uncle Pat's radio was the most amazing means ever for me.

Hearing was seeing on the old radio
When we were young over in Mayo
Michael painted pictures better than sight
We felt the excitement with great delight.

Our ears are our eyes as eager we listen
Player catches the ball to it he did fasten
Brian Carty paints his own, picture unique
As the player goes on, his own score to seek

Voice artists we have, quite a few more
As they tell us about one dramatic score
There's Ger Canning and Darragh Moloney
As out on the pitch they dramatise the story

Cup-a-tea, *crackling* fire, Micháel's radio *waves*

YOU SAY IT BEST

There is a beautiful song out called: 'You say it Best', written by Overstreet and Schlitz, and sung beautifully by Ronan Keating: *'The touch of your hand says you'll catch me whenever I fall. You say it best when you say nothing at all'*. I notice now on television when people are asked a question they almost have to tell you their life story before they answer. Someone said: 'Nowadays we have so much information, know more and more about less and less, until we know nothing about anything'. A little explanation may be needed at times of course.

I did see a Lady once giving short answers, not a 'short' answer, when asked a question. She seemed so confident and relaxed, how refreshing it sounded. Short and to the point is all that's needed. Some people are naturally talkative of course, and that's ok. Anyway, talkative or not, an open mouth and a wagging tongue can get us into all types of trouble. The tongue can be overworked, and can be the most dangerous weapon of all.

What's said may come from the heart, but if the tongue is not rested at times the heart can be overlooked. 'Look before you leap', or in this case 'think before you speak'. Nowadays we have too much communication and not enough communion. We bladder away without thinking what we say. Songs like 'You say it Best', and many others, are the best and most relaxing form of communication.

Communication is a great thing but like any job it takes patience to do it right. I think it should also be a subject in school. The art of communication! Just think of the time and patience an artist puts into his painting. The artist can always change something, but once the tongue says something it's hard to change it. When our mouths are open our ears are naturally closed. We need a good balance, and often for most of us our ears are in great need of exercise.

'Comedy' is a place where the tongue is often at its worst. Laughing from the heart at true comedy is a wonderful thing, but unfortunately what passes for comedy nowadays is often vulgarity. Of course we have audiences who are only too willing to accept and applaud. Is there any comedian out there who is willing to 'stand up' and give us true comedy? Probably the best comedian I ever saw on TV was Tommy Cooper, and he said practically nothing at all. Just like that!

I remember back in the late 1960's, after spending a year in Italy, I could not believe the way the Irish spoke. Could you believe after just one year away I had completely forgotton the Mayo accent. I don't know how I sounded to them with my semi-Italian accent. They trained me back! The gift of speech is a wonderful and necessary gift, but maybe the most abused gift. Just think for a moment about the People who can't speak. Don't we owe it to them to control our tongue at times. Our speech and our accents are all wonderful gifts, but sometimes we say it best when we say nothing at all.

EASY ON THE MAYO

I think it's only recently that people are beginning to discover the beauty of this County. Each county has it's own beauty of course, but Mayo has diversity. While Mayo is known in song as 'the land of the shamrock and heather', Mayo actually means 'Yew', *plain of the Yew,* and do I even know what a Yew Tree looks like? A new adventure awaits me! We see trees of green, but they all have their own uniqueness.

Where would you start with Mayo? We could always start where we live or grew up. Whenever I look out the side window of our house at Donamona I see a wonderful Ring Fort upon the hill. When I look out the front window I see the first snow of winter on Neiphin Mountain. If I climb the hill beside the house I get a wonderful view of Croagh Patrick and the Partry Mountains, and Cnoc-Spudagadain in Manulla. I believe our area is known as *'the plains of mayo'.*

If we live in the town we could start discovering our little streets. Each straight and twisy street must have fascinating histories. Town squares have now been restored in many places. However, they were once hives of activity on market day. One thing I have noticed about those restored Squares is the absence of grass. A little area of green grass, nicely mowed, would enhance those Squares greatly; too much cement. In Castlebar of course we have the beautiful green mall.

Sometimes our local familiar places are the last places we discover. We grew up there so we forget to discover them, but we do eventually get there I think. Mayo has two of the most frequently-visited pilgrimage sights in Ireland, Croagh Patrick and Knock. Two Popes as we know have come to visit Knock, but we will hardly see a Pope climbing 'The Reek'. 'Why not' some may say, and why not indeed. Bishop Michael Neary does it.

When we were young the two places we longed to go to were Pontoon and Lecanvey. Pontoon has Lough Conn, and Lecanvey has Clew Bay. Since then of course we have discovered many beautiful secluded little spots to refresh us, like Keem Bay in Achill for example. Across the water from there we have Blacksod Bay. I believe Mayo has the longest sea-coast in Ireland. Cong decorates the south of the county with its tranquil river and trees branching into Ashford Castle.

The Bog Loop of Clogher attracts many walkers, and evokes memories of all the turf cutting that took place there. Even misty low fields hold their own attraction for some, and the fort upon the hill is a stand out experience for many. So that's a tiny bit of Mayo with it's mountains, sea, lakes, yew trees, shamrock and heather, drumlins, and lowlands. You could write a large book on Mayo, some have, and still not get everything in. My own roots are deep in Mayo soil, but I have discovered recently that one of my great-grandfathers came from Carrownageehy, Milltown, Co Galway. Will Galway bate Mayo? No.

We are young, but our roots are deep
We dream of victory in our sleep
Awakened reality comes with dawn
We carry on, we have a new morn

We follow our team in sunshine or rain
If we lose we have no one to blame
We did our best, there's always tomorrow
Winning next day will drown out our sorrow

Far-away from the land of shamrock and heather
On the big match day we all come together
We kick every ball with our far-away team
It's 'Come on Mayo', let's live the dream

'Up Mayo where ever you go'

BALLINROBE RACES

Most people in Ireland have probably heard of the 'Races of Castlebar'. However, the 'Races of Ballinrobe' is a horse of a different colour. Even though I grew up not many miles from this Race-course I had never visited it, as my interest in horse racing was quite low. I do like horses though, but my memory of them was more of ploughing the land than racing. The Grand-National at Aintree was always an exception of course.

Anyway, being so close to Ballinrobe I decided I should pay a visit to this course. Well I was flabbergasted when I saw how the Race-course had developed. I met Jarleth Reilly there and he told me it was also the first year of the extended Race-track. It was a beautiful sunny evening as horse and riders strove to be the best. It also happened to be Ladies Day when the best dressed is chosen. When it comes to fashion though, or anything maybe, beauty is in the eye of the beholder.

My memory wanders to the past as I notice the roof of a house across the hill. It must be Captain Boycotts I thought. I'm sure he often rode a horse in this field in which we now stood. We were standing in a place that gave a new word to the English language: 'Boycott'. This Land-Captain had a residence on the shores of Lough-mask, and this Race-track on which we stood would have been part of his land.

In 1880 the Irish Land League withdrew labour from Captain Boycott. It was part of the League's campaign for the three F's: 'fair rent', 'fixity of tenure', 'free sale'. The local community stopped harvesting his crops, so he was left isolated. In other words the Tenants 'boycotted' him. Free from work for awhile the People wondered should they give a name to the stand-off. Various names were put forward when a Priest amongst them said: "How about 'Boycott". They all went silent for awhile trying to digest it, but from then on the word 'boycott' became part of the English language. God rest the Captain.

Anyway back to the present and where I'm standing at the Races. My niece Clodagh, as surprised as myself to see me at the races, stops for a few words. She has won a few races herself as a jockey. I watch the Stewards peering through their binoculars to see if any horse is being blocked. "That's not the main reason", Ronan tells me, "the main reason is to check if a horse is going too slow"; saving energy for a more lucrative race later on. How about that! The things you might learn at the races!

In order to feel part of the experience I placed a bet on a horse called 'Must Win'. "I can't lose on this one", I thought. He came close to last, but he might win some day. Horse racing has been taking place on this site, on the Castlebar road, since 1921. However, races have been on-going at different areas of the town since 1774. Anyway I was happy to have finally visited my local Race-Course.

Will I follow the horses now instead of football? I don't think so, but you can build up an interest in anything. The Grand National at Aintree is a race I always follow, and it takes place in the beautiful month of April. History has been made as I write with Rachel Blackmore becoming the first Woman to win the Grand National. It's amazing how a large four-legged animal can jump a fence like Beecher's Brook. Who was the person who thought of such a thing, or was it the horse?. Anyway I should pay a return visit to Ballinrobe Races before I cross my own finishing-line. It's centenary year of this Course as I finish, so 'Race on Ballinrobe.'

Snorting Horses ready on the line
The flag is waved just right on time
Off they go in a swarm like group
Untangle they must or be in the soup

Third fence is here one Rider goes down
The others they jostle each with a frown
It's time to make space as all spread out
Midway now here the crowd give a shout

Just one fence to go, it's now or never
The first three over horses in quiver
One only can win with end-line in sight
A dramatic photo finish, end of the fight.

1916

I often pass the cosy little school at Corduff, Lusk where Thomas Ashe was a teacher. He left all that to fight for an Independent Ireland, and died on hunger strike in England. We are coming to the end of the 'Decade of Centenaries', 2012-2022, which was the period in Irish history culminating in Independence. At the 1916 Rising Padraic Pearse nervously read the Proclamation outside the GPO, with just a few passers-by listening.

From humble beginnings things often have dramatic endings. The 1916 Leaders would say of course that the struggle for freedom started long before them. I'm actually surprised to read how many Protestants Leaders were involved back through the centuries. Sam Maguire for example could not have been a Protestant, could he, he was! We often associate Irish Independence with Catholics, but there were and are Protestant Nationalists. Perhaps the first Taoiseach of a United Ireland will be a northern Protestant. How about that!

There were seven signatories to the Proclamation. Each leaving their own profession, to some degree, to embark on this dangerous journey. The proclamation is a well written document, but I'm not sure about the taking up of arms part. While the 1916 leaders were heroic, is it right to take up arms for any cause? I'm not sure so I'll leave the judgement of that to God. I think the Church speaks of a just war, but I can't imagine Jesus using a gun.

Anyway their actions are now part of our history and has led eventually to an Independent Country; most of our Island at least. 2014 was the 1000 anniversary of the death of Brian Boru at Clontarf. That was the last time we had an Independent United Ireland. Hopefully we will have the same again shortly. Then we can drop that long drawn-out name 'Republic of Ireland' and be called simply and beautifully *'Ireland'*. As the young railway worker, Sean Heuston, stood waiting to be shot in Kilmainham jail he could hardly have for-seen that the main Irish Railway Station would be named after him.

From the 1000 anniversary of 1014 to the 100 anniversary of 1916 we are where we are now, so let's shape the future. Speaking of shape I sometimes think that Ireland has the most beautiful shape of any country in the world. There may be others somewhere I haven't noticed, but unless I'm biased we have the nicest shape. It's the shape of a teddy bear with the North as the Head, Mayo and Galway as the hands and Cork, Kerry Coast as the toes. Some imagination I know!

Eamonn DeValera found himself in Prison after the rising. I read somewhere that while inside he served Mass. Afterwards while the Priest was busy with other things Eamonn melted down the stumps of candles into candle grease. Then he borrowed the Priest's master key and shaped it into the candle grease. He had a photo taken of the shaped key and sent it outside. In came a new copy of the key in the middle of a cake, so with a few others he let himself out. The key to the Presidenc

One of the 1916 Leaders, EamonCeannt, played the uillen pipes for Pope Pius X. The above mentioned Thomas Ashe was co-founder of the Black Raven Pipe band. Willie Pearse was a sculptor and his carvings can be seen on some of the altars in Irish Churches. His brother Padraig set-up a school, to foster the Irish language, which he called St.Enda's. Most of the Leaders seem to have had a strong Faith, and I think they all had the presence of a Priest before they died. Joseph Plunkett got married to Grace on the day of his execution. He wrote beautiful poetry: *I see his blood upon the rose, and in the stars the glory of his eyes.*

I think my Mother was a floating voter, like myself, but she did accept this plaque on behalf of my Father.

ENNIS in 'THE NAUL'

Some might say Ennis is in Clare, and rightly so, but Ennis 'the man' is from 'The Naul'. He has now passed on of course, but as I write this is the centenary year of his birth; 5th May 1919. As well as being the well-known Piper Seamus Ennis was also a singer and a story-teller with a clear voice, he also translated many songs. Through the 'Irish Folklore Commission' he got 2000 Irish songs and dance tunes preserved. That sounds like a very important commission to me.

I remember years ago I drove through 'The Naul', and I thought it a strange place-name. It reminds me of 'The Neale' in Mayo. I think there are very few place names with the word 'The' in front of them. 'The Naul' is anglicised from the Irish 'An Aill', meaning 'The Cliff'. Now I live down the road from this village so I'm making interesting discoveries. It is surrounded by beautiful high hills, rolling hills maybe! It's in Co Dublin, separated from Co Meath by the Delvin River.

Not far away to the north we have the Bellewstown Race-Course upon one of those hills. It must be the highest Race-Course in Ireland, but the horses rise to the occasion. Another interesting place-name nearby is 'Man O War' where coaches stopped off to refresh passengers and horses along the Great Northern Route. That was then! Each place has its own history, and its name is generally taken from that history.

By the way Croke Park pitch, or sod, is grown in 'The Naul', so remember the sowers of the pitch perfect.

Seamus Ennis used a set of pipes which were over 100 years old, picked up cheaply in London. He had them restored and played many a sweet tune for his listeners. Before his death he passed them on to the lovely Piper Liam O'Flynn, now passed away too, 'Tobhair Dom Do Lamh' being the winner here with his piping. These pipes are still going strong as Liam passed them on to Padraic MacMathuna, son of broadcaster Ciaran and Dolly.

Tradition has it that the mastery of the uilleann pipes require seven years learning, seven years practising and seven years playing. The word uilleann comes from the Irish 'Uille', meaning elbow. Coming forward to today we have the young blind Piper, Amy Campbell, here with us in Balbriggan. Going back two hundred years we had another blind Piper Edward K Hyland, who wrote the famous pipes tune 'Fox Chase'

The fox fared better in the following story: Nearby to the east of 'The Naul' we have Gormanstown Castle, which was built in 1786 on the site of an older castle. Each time a Head of the household died foxes came to congregate under the window of the dying or dead Viscount. They stayed around the castle until the funeral was over and then returned to their normal habitat. It seems to have started in the 17th century when the Viscount Gormanstown saved the lives of a fox and her cubs. Interesting! Gormanstown Castle became a boarding school in 1955, run by the Franciscan Order.

Seamus Ennis seems to have been the inspiration of many a traditional musician. Maybe even the Lady that can make the accordian talk, Sharon Shannon. There is now a beautiful Centre dedicated to his memory in The Naul, 'The Seamus Ennis Centre'. Remember he was playing at a time when traditional music was not that popular. He kept at it though until the great revival. Actually I'd like to see Bagpipes being played more often in Croke Park, a lovely outdoor instrument! There is an International 'Uilleann Piping Day' on October 20th each year, so the Pipes may be calling you!

The calm before the sound

ISRAEL

Why Israel? Well I would find it hard to pick out any other Country as there are so many. Israel is the land of the Jews, and they are the 'chosen' people in the Bible. Now I wouldn't know as much as the scholars about this Nation but I did a little research. If we look for Israel on the map it's hard to find it's so small, but what a fascinating history this Jewish Nation has. So this little story of Israel is for the 'ordinary man on the street' like myself, if there are any such people nowadays.

100 years ago the present-day Israel did not exist and now it's one of the most modern States in the World. Theodor Herzl and a group of exiled Jews held a congress in Berne, Switzerland in 1897. At that time Herzl wrote in his diary: "Today I founded the Jewish State. If I said this out loud I would be met with universal laughter". However 50 years later the Jewish State of Israel was set up. Here we are speaking about the modern State of Israel, but we must go back.

In the Bible story Abraham was the founder of the Jewish people in 2000 BC, he is actually mentioned outside the Bible too in history. His Grandson Jacob was given the name Israel by God. Because of a famine the Israelites found themselves in exile in Egypt. In 1500 BC Moses led them back to their own land of Canaan (Palestine), but made a prophecy they would loose their land later because of their disobedience to God.

In 1000 BC David conquered Jeruslaem and prophesied the coming of the Messiah. His Son Solomon built the Temple. In 600 BC the Babylonian King conquered Jerusalem, and destroyed the Temple. The Israelites were exiled to Babylon for 70 years. They returned under the Persian Emperor, and the second Temple was then built in Jerusalem. Then Alexander the Great conquered the Persian Empire in 300 BC and Israel became a province within the Greek Empire. Finally in 100 BC the Roman Empire takes over in Israel. Then Jesus is born!

Jesus was born into the Jewish religion, but obviously he was also the first Christian. Pope John Paul called the Jews 'The Elder Brothers of the Church'. Those Jews who have not received Jesus as the Messiah gather at the Western Wall, *the wailing wall, to* pray for the coming of their Messiah and the restoration of the Temple. Some Jews think that time is near as they have now come full circle and formed their own State again, after 2000 years in exile.

Anyway back to the time-line: In 70 AD the Jews rebelled against being under the Roman Empire. They lost, so Jerusalem was destroyed and the second Temple was burned down. Jews were not allowed to stay in their own land, so they were dispersed across the Roman Empire and beyond. This was the third Jewish exile and they ended up in many countries World-Wide. After 2000 years in exile most of the Jews had accepted their fate. They became part of whatever country they had settled in. Then came Theodor Herzl and his vision of a return.

The Jews returned and Israel was reborn, on the 14th May
1948, when David Ben-Gurion read the declaration of
Independence in Tel-Aviv. President Truman of America
accepted the new State of Israel on the same day. What a
journey! This was obviously very difficult for the
Palestinians who had now to share the Land with the new
state of Israel. In some ways the Jews were just returning
to their own land; but after 2000 years! Different Arab
countries are now beginning to accept Israel. There is still
tensions between Israel and Palestine. People are hoping
for a peaceful final two State solution.

Palestine is divided into two parts at the moment, the
West Bank and the Gaze Strip are divided by the land of
Israel. It would be nice to see both parts become united.
Israel would have to give a piece of land where the two
'Palestines' are separated, in return for part of the West
Bank further north. If Israel is small the Gaza Strip is
tiny, but there are 1.5 million people living there. It is
also strategically positioned beside the Mediterranean
Sea. Even though it's in dispute by both sides the
American President has now, in 2020, accepted Jerusalem
as the Capital of Israel.

If as some Jews believe now might be the time for the
coming of their Messiah, might he not be the same
Messiah whom Christian Jews accepted 2000 years ago,
and are now awaiting his return. There is only one
Messiah and we await his awesome arrival. The World
needs him now, as it always did. Come Lord Jesus, do not
delay.

Awesome Galilee, by the tranquil Sea
Storms left behind humans to unwind

Two thousand years ago amidst the chopping sea
Humans feared and wept, the Master calmly slept

'Why are you afraid, am I not with you
Calm there *stormy* sea, let my friends here be'

Sea of Galilee

THE '*SWINGING*' '60'S

They say if you were a Teenager in the 1960's you never grew up, I better make a start so. Actually I've only just realized something about the word Teenager. Teen (Deag) years start at 11 in Irish, aon-deag go dti naoi-deag. They also start at 11 in Italian actually (Dici), un-dici is eleven in Italian. Does that mean other Nations mature faster than the English, ah no. Anyway let's get back to the swinging 60's as they were called by some.

Swinging was not the right word for some of the things that happened in the 1960's. Tensions were rising in Northern Ireland. We had an ugly Vietnam war on-going, and we had the Cuban Missile Crisis. President Kennedy was assassinated in 1963. Later on in the decade Martin Luther King and Bobby Kennedy were both assasinated in 1968. King said in a famous speech: *"I've been to the mountain and seen the other side, mine eyes have seen the glory of the coming of the Lord"*, amazing words! Premonition maybe, as shortly after that he was shot.

King also said: "Justice is indivisible, injustice anywhere is a threat to justice everywhere". Those words are worth thinking about. President Johnson signed into law the civil rights act of 1964 and the voting rights act in 1965. Kennedy had earlier created 'The Peace Corps' to help smaller developing Nations. Pope John XX111, who had started the second Vatican Council, also died in 1963. Each decade has its own troubles of course, and the 'swinging' '60's did not escape. Humanity has tried and failed so many times, but have we learned anything?

The 1960's was the time of The Beatles, Elvis Presley and Cliff Richard. I liked Cliff at that time but it was only in later years I got to like the voice of Elvis and songs of The Beatles. One song I did like in the 1960's was: 'I'm a Believer' sung by the Monkees. Interestingly enough that song was written by Neil Diamond, a wonderful singer himself. The Irish Dancehalls were in full *swing* during the 1960's, and the mineral bar was doing a roaring trade. Most teenagers were pioneers, meaning they did not drink alcohol. People 'grew up' then, or so they thought, and the Lounge Bars took over.

The cassette tape, remember that, was invented in Holland in 1963, and something called 'The Internet' was used by the US Military in 1969. The heart Pace-Maker was invented in 1961 by Wilson Greatbatch. Later on in the decade Christian Barnard carried out the first heart transplant. The Soviet Union actually were the first to put a man, Yuri Gagarin, into space. They were also the first to land a spacecraft on the Moon, but the US got their man there first

While the 1960's were known as the 'swinging sixties' each individual had her/his own worries to deal with. So people were not always swinging to the 60's! It was a time of change and we don't often like change, but it's part of living. Change for the sake of change is not good, but change for a good reason is very good. Let's not swing too far too fast or we might have a nasty fall. While some things change other sound things never change. I suppose we are changing all the time anyway, maybe not as dramatic as the caterpillar into the butterfly though. We might have to wait till after death for that.

Stuck in between the 1950's and 1970's I suppose 1960 was an interesting decade. However Life is what you make it no matter which decade you live in. 'Up's and Down's' there always will be in this life, but we must try and see the glass half full. The parting glass will come soon enough! Sixty years have passed since 1960, and this 2020 is the first decade of the rest of our lives, so let's live the life we were born to live with all its swings and arrows. President Kennedy didn't live to see his pronouncement come to pass of 'landing a man on the Moon, and returning him safely to earth, before the decade is out'. That awesome thing did happen in1969.

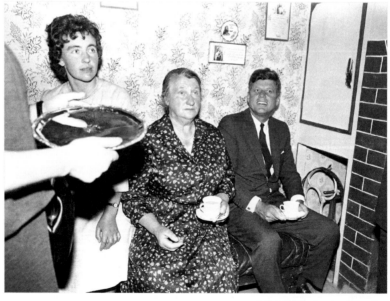

(Irish Photo Archive)

"Ah, just a cup in me hand"

MAN ON THE MOON

Today as I write, 20th July 2019, is the 50th anniversary of Man's first landing on the Moon. I have been glued, not super-glue, to the TV because I find it a fascinating thing. I was in Italy at the time of the landing and I thought I was far away, but the Moon! I sometimes glance up and try to imagine man landing there. What type of Person would risk their life by going to the Moon I wonder. Neil Armstrong, Michael Collins and 'Buzz Aldrin' did, others followed later.

Actually after reading Neil Armstrong's life story I have come to the conclusion that landing on the Moon was just another step for him. He was a Pilot in the US/Japan war, and that was risky as many did not return. He and a group of other astronauts had to test out so many things before they even got into space. They started as pilots zooming up to the edge of space. Others broke through where they felt as light as a feather. Actually it took 400,000 people to get man to the moon eventually. Can you imagine if just one of them slipped up!

While the two walked on the Moon Michael Collins had a lonely journey orbiting around it until their return. If anything went wrong he would have had to return to the Earth alone, leaving his two friends stranded. It doesn't bear thinking about! He would be tempted to try and rescue them I'm sure, but it would probably be beyond his reach. He'd be so near yet so far away. Anyway he was a relieved man when they docked back. Heading home is always nice.

Buzz Armstrong brought some bread and wine and held a religious service in the capsule before exiting on to the surface. They had to come back down to earth of course, and life would never again be the same for them. Facing the media day in day out was not easy. Neil had a great gift of speech though; to the point! He said that the Earth is like a spaceship, with people on the outside instead of the inside. He's right, as the Earth orbits the Sun just like the spaceship orbited the Moon, and of course the Moon orbits the Earth. We are all in orbit!

Neil said when he was a boy he sometimes had dreams of flying just above the ground. I also had the same type of dream, and it's a lovely feeling, but then I'd wake up and it was firmly back to earth. Maybe there's a lost astronaut in me! I must say I just love to see the thin rim of a new Moon, but I may not venture any further than earth. When Janet Armstrong, Neil's wife, was asked what she felt when her husband hopped on to the Moon she said: "Out of this World!" Some years earlier they had to deal with the passing of their daughter Karen at the tender age of three. Neil must have felt close to her on the Moon

Some will tell you that the Moon is part of the earth, which broke away from us long ago. Does that mean our ancestors were on the moon before us? They say Mars is next, so where will it end. In our galaxy alone we also have Neptune, Venus, Jupiter, Mercury, Uranus, Saturn, and the Sun to keep us warm. So there is no shortage of work for the scientists, one step at a time of course. The rest of us have enough to be thinking about down here. If the Irish ever set up a pub on the red planet it will surely be called: 'The Irish Mars Bar'.

THE ROSARY PRIEST

The teenager Patrick waved goodbye to his Parents from their cottage, with tears in his eyes, under the Ox mountains at Carracastle, Mayo. If you go to nearby Attymas now you will find a beautiful Centre with his name 'Fr Peyton Memorial Centre'. It's a big change from his thatched cottage to this Centre, but our lives move on in different ways. In between Fr Peyton became the best known Irishman in the World, and maybe the greatest evangeliser of the twentieth century.

In the world of today you would hardly expect the best known Irishman to be an evangeliser unless he became Pope. That is something that could happen some time, and would not be a surprise. Anyway, before his ordination Patrick became ill with tuberculosis and came close to death. His doctor told him the only hope was to pray. He did that and asked Our Lady to intercede for his recovery, He promised that if he lived he would proclaim the value of the Family Rosary. He made a full recovery.

He had now to keep his promise, but how? In 1942 he founded the 'Family Rosary Crusade' in Albany, New York. He set up a half-hour weekly radio Prayer Programme, on one of the top Stations in America. It may be no coincidence that his first programme was on the 13th May, the feast-day of Our Lady of Fatima who is also 'Our Lady of the Rosary'. His departure from his home was on that date too.

He got top Holywood stars like Bing Crosby and Grace Kelly to present some of his programmes. He then founded 'Family Theatre' in 1947, and the first programme was hosted by the actor James Stewart. Fr Peyton also went around the world preaching the Family Rosary in large stadiums. He drew a crowd of 75,000 to the Polo Grounds in New York, 80,000 to Wembley Stadium in London, 250,000 to the Golden Gate Park in San Francisco, and two million to both San Paolo Brazil and Manila in the Phillippines. I'm sure he often thought of his own tranquil spot under the Ox mountains

The writer of this book was born on the feast-day of the Holy Rosary, but I do recall asking Br. Aloysius what was the purpose of repeating all those Hail Mary's. We were on an Aer Lingus jet high above the clouds, above all places. He gave me the best answer I have heard on the recitation of the rosary. He said great saints can lift their minds automatically to God, but us normal human beings need something to keep our minds meditated; hence the rosary.

The origin of the Rosary is unclear but, according to Catholic Tradition, Our Lady appeared to St Dominic and presented him with the Rosary herself. This happened in the 13th century, and it was developed as time went on. It was based on the Angel Gabriels visit to Mary at the Annunciation. The word rosary means 'Rose Garden' from the Latin 'Rosarium'. A legend says that when the monks prayed the 'Hail Marys' a garland of roses was formed in Marys hands.

People gathered around the fire-place, on their knees, saying the rosary is a big part of Irish history. If we don't say it now I don't think it's because we are great saints. Locally Jim Bourke from Ballydavoc led us in the rosary at Donamona Grotto. It's a nice image to hold in the memory from other days as the words 'Hail Mary' echoed through the nearby castle. We don't hear the word 'beads' used much now if at all. Both the prayers and the beads are used as 'Rosary'. I like to keep on with the beads. Fr Patrick Peyton was named 'Mayo Person of the Year' for 1987. He had a saying: 'The Family that prays together stays together'.

HOW ARE THINGS IN DONAMONA

Is that old castle still standing there, and what about the Donamona fair. Some of you will know that the real words are *'How are things in Glocca Morra, is that little brook still leaping there. Does it still run down to Donna cove, is that willow tree still weeping there'.* That nostalgic song was written by Yip Harburg with melody by Burton Lane. We love to look back in song to see what was then but may be no more now, such is life!

What songs might the Irish be listening to before the showband era of the 'swinging' 60's. Well we already had Radio Luxembourg, but from an Irish perspective we had quite a few singers. One singer who stood out for me personally in the 50's was Willie Brady. He had a lovely voice but passed away at the young age of 38. Delia Murphy from Mayo and Margaret Barry from Cork had very distinctive voices in those days of our youth. Two other names I remember singing at that time were Brendan O'Dowda and Michael O'Duffy.

Before we had singers we had to have composers of course. Galway Bay was written by Arthur Colahan with melody by John Huggard. Frank O'Donovan, Batty Brennan from the Riordans, wrote 'Sitting on the Bridge below the Town', sung by Joe Lynch. Frank also wrote 'On the One Road' which the Irish Army made their own. Francis Fahy from Kinvara wrote 'My Own Dear Galway Bay', and 'The auld plaid shawl.

Percy French wrote 'The Mountains of Mourne' which quite a few singers have sung. He created a great nostalgic image for us at that particular time: *'You remember young Peter O'Loughlin of course, well he's over here with the rest of the force. I met him today I was crossing the strand, and he stopped all the traffic with a wave of his hand. And as we stood talking of days that are gone, the whole population of London looked on. But for all his great powers he's wishful to be, where the Mountain of Mourne sweep down to the sea'*

Leo Maguire composed 'Dublin can be Heaven', which Noel Purcell made his own in song. Leo it was who told us every week on Radio: 'If you feel like singing, do sing an Irish song'. Richard Farrelly wrote the 'Isle of Innisfree', which was interwoven into the film 'The Quiet Man'. Female singers of that time were Bridie Gallagher and Maisie McDaniels who may also have ventured into the 60's. We also had Eileen Donaghy and Ruby Murray. In classical we had Castlebar's Margaret Burke Sheridan and of course John McCormack from Athlone.

Singer Patrick O'Hagan was father of Johnny Logan. Even Dinjo got in on the act of singing with 'The Connemara Bus'. *It passes each day down the village street, is there any chance of a vacant seat, There might now so thanks be to God, for the Connemara bus.* Two 'local' men who had wonderful voices were Brose Walsh Belcarra singing amongst other songs the 'Red River Valley', and Peter Murphy Clogher singing 'The Boys in Blue'. Local is also Universal, so it's hard to beat local!

IT'S THE PLACE WHERE I LIVE
(Melody with Author)

It's the place where I live, the place where I give
To friend and to foe, and everyone I know
Wherever I roam, it's the place I call home
Donamona in Mayo, where ever I may go

Our village holding memories, old Castle standing there
The local shop now empty, but the Pub is going fare
Donamona Fair moved on now, to towns of greater size
But our Village holds its dignity, that's the greater prize.

It's the Place where I Live etc. ....

The Crossroads in the centre, branching where it may
West to Ballintubber, Clogher school along the way
Northwards on to Castlebar, Belcarra Chapel on the hill
Along the road to Balla , Guesdian Graveyard lies so still

Then the road to Ballyglass, where soccer is the game
Win this game or lose it, the playing is the name.
So when you go a-travelling, where ever you may go
Remember where you came from, that spot in old Mayo

It's the place where I live, the place where I give
To friend and to foe, and everyone I know
Wherever I roam, it's the place I call home
Donamona in Mayo, wherever I may go,

THE TURKEY EGG

Is there such a thing as a turkey egg now-a-days. I suppose there has to be if there are turkeys, but you would never hear of a turkey egg now. Not so when I was young because sometimes my supper would be a turkey egg. Now it wasn't just a case of putting down the egg to boil, as first I had to go in search of the egg. Working for my supper! I doubt if I would eat a turkey egg now, it is much larger than the hen egg and has brown spots if my memory is correct. They were egg-ceptional.

My Mother used to rare some turkeys for Christmas, and then my Father took them in his van to market and sell them. The turkeys thought they were just 'going out' for Christmas, but there was no return. I have said it before that I must become a vegetarian, but I keep putting it on the long finger. "Well do it then and stop talking or writing about it", some might say. "ok!"

Anyway some of our turkeys would decide to lay their eggs in the neighbouring field. This field was full of bushes, so it was a struggle to solve the jigsaw puzzle of finding the egg for supper, not always laid in the same spot I must add. The adventure was fantastic though, and there was many a scramble through the bramble. Once finally found, sometimes in the dark, their was great relief and supper was secured. Food-wise I always thought an egg was different than other foods, in the sense that it's part of an animal, or foul, but doesn't diminish the foul.

Other memories of those times, in the sunshine of our happy youth, would be going to the vegetable market in Castlebar, held in Market Square above all places. Also going to the pig and calf market in Rush street, and the large fair in the Fair green. Turkeys arriving at any of those places was a rare sight. "What are those two-legged things?", said the pig to the calf. "They are turkeys", said the calf. "What are they doing here", asked the pig. "They come every Christmas to be sold for dinner", said the calf. "That's terrible", said the pig, "I wouldn't like that happening to me". The calf grinned.

Cattle looing, sheep maaing
Pigs grunting, goats baaing.
Farmers selling, are you buying
Jobbers checking, are you lieing

Here now, I'll give you fifty
No, no, it must be sixty
I don't know, it seems a lot
Just look, see what you've got

Walking on, meet the neighbour
Have a chat, about the weather
Hearty laughter hangs in the air
Many sounds found at the Fair

2020 VISION

Yes we have reached 2020, and my memory wanders to the past, again! Well it's beyond my memory really, but it concerned me. My great-grand father, James Kilcourse, wandered across his fields at Guesdian to the river. On the other side he saw a young lady, Mary Mullin, coming down the hill from Welshpool. They had a chat across the river, and eventually no river would stop them becoming man and wife.

They set up home at Fairhill, and had about seven children. The Kilcourse name has died out locally now, but there may be some of that name in America. There are I know some cousins in Philadelphia, but I don't know if any of them has the Kilcourse name, must check! I was watching the 'Back to the Future' film on TV during Christmas and the young man, Marty, was desperate to get his Parents together so that he could get back to his present life. He got back!

If the river had blocked my great-grandparents that time at Guesdian I may now be asking myself 'who do you think you are'. I may have had to come here through a different route. We can still ask that question because we are much more than we think we are. We are part of our past generations body-wise, with our own uniqueness of course. Soul-wise we are much more again, more than we can imagine. *"But what we are to be in the future has not yet been revealed"*

Back to the present now and 2020 is an interesting number. It's 100 years since we had 1919 when the Irish Nation was in birth pangs, we escaped all that. We may still be suffering the after-effects of course. In another 100 years we will have 2121 whatever that may bring. In between those 200 years most of us will have come and gone. At this moment some are entering the conveyor belt of life while others are departing, hopefully headed in the right direction.

Sometime during 2019 my brother made up a joke about the upcoming year of 2020. One man asked the other: "Where do you see yourself in a year's time?" The other man responded: "How am I supposed to know, I don't have 2020 vision", that was it! We told my brother he'll have to do better, he will have to adjust his visor. We all need revision at the end or beginning of each year, the mind's visor can become cloudy so it must be cleaned and revised.

2020 is a good roundy number, it's a leap year, but it's just another year. The present year is of course the most important as it's the only year we can live right now. 'What's another year', sang Johnny Logan. Well, it depends on us doesn't it. Then again it seems this year may not totally depend on us. The Covid-19 has arrived and has already changed things dramatically. It's a World-wide thing and it has stopped us in our tracks. Covid19 will be etched on the mind for 2020, but hopefully other things will be remembered.

THE LITTLE FLOWERS

The 'Little Flower' is the name given to a young French Saint, 'Therese of Lisieux', young in the sense that she died at the age of 24. I wonder how she would fit into the modern world where people demand their rights. She welcomed any suffering that came her way without complaint. She offered it up, which might be something missing in today's world. When we reach rock bottom, which we all do, it's a great relief to say 'I'll offer this up' for myself, and maybe more importantly for others.

Now I do believe that people have a right not to be walked on, but having all your rights does not take away suffering. The World needs people like St Therese who may not fit in at times, but who may be the 'salt of the earth'. Salt has got a bad name recently, but maybe it's 'too much' that should have the bad name not the salt itself. A sprinkling of salt in food, and especially in life, can make a difference.

Therese Martin, St Therese of Lisieux, was born on 2nd. January 1873, and she died of tuberculosis on the 30th September 1897. She was the youngest of nine children, and her Mother died when she was four. What a wrench! She was a girl who wanted everything until her conversion on Christmas Eve at age 14. After that she wanted nothing but to love God and people.. She said: "What we need is great love not great deeds". To do the ordinary things with extraordinary love!

St Therese loved snow and flowers and she saw herself as a little flower, by being her little self, among all the other flowers in God's garden. Hence, she became known as 'The Little Flower'. "My mission", she said, "to make God loved, will begin after my death. I will spend my heaven doing good on earth, I will let fall a shower of roses". There are two Irish child saints, not canonised, who like St Therese both lost their Mothers in early childhood. Tuberculosis, or something similar, was also the cause of death in these two cases.

Kathleen Kilbane from Achill, spent the last years of her life in a Sanitorium at Ballinrobe. She was the youngest patient there, but made a great impression in the things she said about God to the staff and other patients. She made an interesting promise before she died: "If anybody hears about me and likes me I will help them to be always good". Kathleen died on the same day as this writer was born, 7th October 1947, at the age of 13. A beautiful large white rose, found growing in an unusual place, was plucked and entwined between her fingers.

Nellie Organ from Cork had a great devotion to the Holy Eucharist. So much so that she got a special dispensation to receive Communion at the age of four, shortly before she died. In fact it is widely acknowledged that the life of this little girl was responsible for Pope St Pius X reducing the age for first Communion, down from twelve years to seven. From the testimony of Staff of the Good Shepherd Convent she had great conversations with 'Holy God', as she called him. Nellie also loved flowers.

Back to 'The Little Flower' herself who kept a diary, and it was from her writings that her spirituality became known. Her autobiography, written under obedience, called 'Story of a Soul' is read the world over. She was canonised by Pope Pius X1 on 17th May 1925, and was declared a 'Doctor of the Church' by Pope John Paul 11 in 1997; the only Doctorate of his pontificate. All that for 24 years of hidden life! She is the Saint of the Missions, and her feast day is on 1st October. So when things go wrong don't forget to 'offer it up', and then go and smell the flowers.

A flower *scent* is Heaven *sent*

THE SANATORIUM

It's interesting that when I looked-up Sanatoriums, what appeared was Hotels and Guest Houses. A far cry from the image we have of Sanatoriums of not so long ago! Maybe the word Sanatorium is OK for Hotels too as it's meaning, from the Latin, is 'health-giving'. A nice break in a good Hotel can be health-giving. Anyway the Sanatoriums I write about here are quite different from a Hotel. A lot of people suffering from tuberculosis (TB) spent the last years of their lives in Sanatoriums.

They had the same effect as this present-day covid 19 with people keeping apart. It's different than the Nursing homes of today though as here visitors are afraid of giving the disease, back then they were afraid of getting it. While nobody wanted to be in the Sanatorium, and few wanted to visit, it was good to have them. The nurses and doctors then too put their own lives at risk. The only sanatiser being soap and water, good to have that too.

Irish government minister Dr. Noel Brown played a big part in looking after TB patients as Minister for Health. He set up a Sanatorium at Creagh House in his native Ballinrobe. A lovely wooded area owned originally by the Knox Family! The patients there were mostly immigrant workers who had returned from employment in Scotland and England. Employment then was outdoors in all types of weather. Dr Brown's own Parents died from the disease and he caught the disease himself.

Tuberculosis is believed to be thousands of years old. 10,000 people a year died from TB in Dublin in the late 1940's. It went into the lungs and bones, and was no respecter of age as young and old died from it. It was a sad lonely painful death, but the Sanatorium had their own little community of suffering together. Each generation has it's own sicknesses and viruses to deal with. In the generation before mine, early 20th century, we had quite a few.

The one that stands out of course is 'The Spanish Flu', which had nothing at all to do with Spain as it did not originate there. It was estimated by the World Health Organisation (WHO) to have claimed the lives of upwards on 50 million people world-wide. Cancer is still with us, and while not a virus as such it can be caught from certain viruses. Another Bacterial disease was Diphtheria which affected the throat. 'Disease' is an apt word because dis-ease is indeed what we feel.

My own personal memory of diseases as a child was that of measles, mumps and whooping cough. 'Draw back, Draw back' we all shouted when one of us started a fit of coughing. For some reason we kept coughing for a long time without taking a breath. When the draw-back did come you could hear our relief. With measles we broke out in small red spots or bumps, a bit like rubella later on. The mumps gave us swollen puffy cheeks. Just found out that the MMR vaccine covers the three above: measles, mumps, rubella. Anyway, a modern day sanatorium is a hotel and spa. Things change all the time!

FAVOURITE DAYS

It's Thursday as I write this and it's still my favourite day. It's amazing how we associate different days of the week with different feelings. Many people don't like Monday, but I feel great on a Monday. Maybe it's from the rest on Sunday. Chris Cristofeson sang of feeling alone on a Sunday morning sidewalk: *'there's something in a Sunday that makes a body feel alone'*. I actually like Sunday morning because of Mass, but in the afternoon I feel a bit depressed at times.

Thursday is my day as I said, maybe from the time I had a half day off work when I worked in Castlebar. I think the Connaught Telegraph came out on a Thursday in those times, so I must have liked reading that. Tuesday and Friday might be my least favourite days. It's all to do with association, but we can change ourselves to feel differently. However it's amazing how we keep slipping back into the routine and feeling of a certain day.

I don't think we have favourite weeks unless it's Christmas or Easter. Favourite months maybe, but we do certainly have favourite Seasons. I must say I never really liked the Summer as much as the other seasons, maybe it's because the routine is gone and I feel unsettled. As for holidays they can be a torture, but the after effects can be good I suppose. In other words holidays interfere with my equelibrium. It should possibly be the other way around maybe.

My favourite season is Autumn when things become settled again. The leaves are turning to gold and falling on our heads with a gentle breeze. It's a time for meditation, and maybe thinking of the next life. October is my favourite month, but I do like the whole period from then to Christmas. I wonder do we die a little during winter, so thank God for Christmas. We spring into Spring when everything starts to blossom again.

I notice the Weather People have changed their winter season to start in December, even though it's officially November. I would change it further still for winter to start in January, as the coldest months in general are January, February and March. That's my experience anyway, but of course the darkest nights are in November, December and January. So we can't have it every way. I do recall my Mother saying winter is from 21st December to 21st March. Weather-wise she was indeed wise.

Anyway back to the Days, and we also have favourite times of the day. The morning is my best time. My Father used to say you get twice as much done in the first half of the day as you do in the second half. An interesting observation I must say. Somebody said everything is just a feeling, so why should one feeling be better, or worse, than any other feeling. We have our feelings about each day, and each time of the day, but they are all just feelings. Maybe we are rejecting some feeling because it is not as 'good' as the feeling we had yesterday. Of course our actions can transform our feelings!

Perhaps 'one day at a time' is all about accepting the feelings of that day, and making the best of them. We should rule the day, but sometimes we let the day rule us. We might have to attack some days, while other days just go in a flow with us. I heard someone say: 'If you are sad for an hour you are missing 60 minutes of happiness'. That's going a bit too far I suppose as sadness we will have, but the gist of the saying may be true. No doubt amongst the 'normal' we will have some bizarre days.

'Hay' there! A Day is what you make it'.

DAYS BAZAAR

My stories so far have come from west and east so here is one from the midlands. Mullingar, An Muileann gCearr, means: 'The Incorrect Mill'. It went anti-clockwise for some reason. The river must be flowing the wrong way, or was it the wind. Anyway that's the meaning given for this midland town. As a teenager my Mother worked in a 'Newsagents' in Mullingar called 'Days Bazaar'. I don't know what a Newsagents is called nowadays, maybe just a shop that sells newspapers amongst other things.

The Owners of 'Days Bazaar' at that time were the Canavan Sisters, May and Lena, from Brize, Balla. They were first-cousins of my Grand-Mother so they invited my Mother up for a year to help in their shop. Interestingly enough it might have been as easy to get to Mullingar then as now. The Mayo train passed through Mullingar at that time, but it takes a different line now. You could board at Manulla, just a short walk away in those days, and off with ya.

'Days Bazaar' is still in Mullingar, but it's now a coffee shop. Originally it was founded by Charles Day in 1879, as a General Store. He stayed in business for 50 years. May Canavan then took over the shop, and she also stayed in business for about 50 years. She then returned to her native Mayo with her sister Lena. It then passed into the hands of Jim and Miriam O'Donnell, for maybe another 40 or 50 years.

The present owners are Adrian and Deirdre Murphy from Co. Tyrone. They it was who turned the Bazaar into a coffee shop. They might continue the tradition of staying in business for 50 years, as the others have, one day at a time though! It would be interesting if The Knight Family called into Days Bazaar, maybe they have. Like many other businesses all coffee shops are closed as I write, because of the covid19. Hopefully they will be open as you read this.

Mullingar is the capital town of County Westmeath, and it's also a Cathedral town. The Bishop of Meath lives here. I hope the Mill wheel is still rolling along nicely, one way or the other. Joe Dolan automatically comes to mind when we hear of this town being mentioned. I don't know if he had a song about the mill, or any mill. The last time I was in Days Bazaar I met his brother Ben there. Joe had some lovely songs in the olden days like: 'Pretty Brown Eyes', 'The Answer to Everything' and 'My Own Peculiar Way'.

That's Day's Bazaar in the midland town of Mullingar. Since the driving ban on alcohol coffee has come into its own, and that's no bad thing. Coffee comes now in many forms: cappucino, latte (mostly milk), americano, which is a plain coffee, and probably the same as an 'Irishano' People will always be pulling off the highway roads for a break in their long journeys. So if do you happen to be passing, day or night, drop in to Days Bazaar for a coffee of some form. You will be drinking in its history, and a bit of mine.

VACANCIES

(*Job Offer 1*)

Young Person wanted as Sales Rep,
             good wages and great future prospects.
Company car for work and personal use,
             expenses paid including all meals.
Four weeks holiday every year,
             one further week at Christmas and Easter.
Monthly bonuses and career breaks,
             you will have lots of Admirers in this job.
Parties for customers every month,
             your friends will be many and varied.
Through 'cleverness' you will possess the World,
             now come and join us.

             Signed: *Jonathan*
             Motoronics International

"Hmmm, who in their right mind would 'turn down' a job offer like this?" Some do.

....

(*Job Offer 2*)

Young person wanted as sales Rep,
             wages not of this life.
You may be homeless at Christmas,
             agony and 'joy' at Easter.

Your friends and admirers may be few,
         you will be like lambs among wolves.
Courage needed, but through perseverance
         you will possess your own selves.
  Your parties will be prayer,
         your holidays are your rest periods.
You will be hated by many on account of my name,
         now come follow me.

Signed: *Jesus*
Kingdom of Heaven

"Hmmm, who in their right mind would 'accept' a job offer like this?"   Some do.

"Go Pasture my Sheep"

THE FAR EAST

The far east started very much in the near west, in Donamona and Belcarra, Co Mayo to be exact. Fr John Blowick started a missionary order called: 'The Maynooth Mission to China', later to be called 'The Society of St Columban'. He was the son of a Donamona girl, Nora Madden, and a Belcarra chap Johnny Blowick. They got married and eventually John was born on the 26th October 1888.

On this date, 19th March 1920, exactly 100 years ago, the now Fr John accompanied 15 Priests to Hanyang China to start the mission.He wanted to stay in China but he had to return and build up the Order in Ireland. Bishop Galvin of Cork was co-founder, as he had already spent some time in China. To bring Christianity to China was a daring thing to do, but worth any sacrifice to them. 'Fortune favours the brave', but this is a different kind of fortune than is normally understood.

The Columban Order today have their Head-house at Dalgan Park, Navan. The name Dalgan Park actually came from Shrule, somewhere on the border-line of Galway and Mayo. It was here that Fr John set up his first house for the training of young men for their journey to China. The Order stayed at Shrule for 23 years and in those years 333 Priests and Brothers went to preach the Gospel in foreign Lands. That house at Shrule is now gone I think but the memories live on.

Fr John Blowick started a magazine called: 'The Far East' to make known his work, and collect some funds. I would say that most family homes in Ireland purchased a monthly copy of 'The Far-East'. It was in the dresser with the cups and saucers. It did not have much competition, as the magazines that flood the market nowadays did not exist. At a certain point the Missionary Order members had to leave China, but the Columban Order developed in other Countries.

In 1922 Fr John founded the 'Columban Missionary Sisters' with the help of Lady Maloney. He was encouraged also in that endeavour by Marcella Fitzgerald Kenny of Clogher House; another near west connection. Even to get to China in those days must have been an ordeal in itself. Some have made the ultimate sacrifice for the cause. One Columban Sister, Joan Sawyer, and twenty Priests have suffered the death penalty. It's a changed world now, and we are more likely to have Chinese Priests coming to Ireland than vice versa.

The Irish went to convert the world, and now the world is coming to convert the Irish. I suppose there's a certain humility needed for that, but sure it's good for us. At the time of Fr John Blowick's death in 1972 the Order had almost 1000 members. And so when Nora Madden and Johnny Blowick married they could hardly have foreseen the expanding internatioal wripple that their union had created. The Belcarra Far-East flag is kept flying with Sr Mary O'Malley Lisiniskea, Fr Martin Bourke Roslahan and Fr Frank Nally Fairhill.

LOLEK

Lolek's Mother was a frail woman who had lost her daughter Olga in infancy. When he arrived, six years after his sister's passing, he brought her great joy. At the moment of birth she asked the midwife to open the windows so that the first sounds her son Lolek would hear were the singing of vespers to Our Lady from the Church across the road. Nine years later she passed away at the age of forty-five. That was the first wrench of Lolek's young life.

Lolek had a brother, Edmund, thirteen years older than himself. In spite of the gap in age, maybe because of it, they were great friends and Edmund brought him on many of his adventures. Football and skiing were high on the list. Edmund went on to study medicine and became a doctor to the delight of Lolek and his Father. The delight was short lived as Edmund contracted scarlet fever while trying to save a patient with the same disease.

We can only imagine Lolek's pain when his brother died, at the age of 24, just three years after his Mother. Now there was just left his Father and himself, aged twelve, but they got-on well together. Pushing back the furniture they played football inside their apartment, no VAR allowed. There was a Jewish Community in the town and a football match was sometimes organised against the Christians. On a few occasions the Jewish goalkeeper was absent so Lolek stood in for the Jewish team.

When war broke out and some Nazi's entered Lolek's country from the west he got a job breaking stones in a quarry. Eight hour days at such work was not easy for a teenager, coupled by the fact that food was rationed. A coffee break was a luxury of luxuries, and he kept going mostly in silence. He also realised that others had it much worse than himself. After some months he was transferred to a factory job, and that gave him great relief. Lolek then joined compulsory military training but refused to fire or even hold a gun. How he managed to get out of that we don't really know.

In the midst of all his hardship Lolek came home one day to find his Father had died. He is heart broken, and at the age of just twenty is the only member left of his immediate Family. So with each wrench of losing every member of his family one wonders how he survived after that. 'What's to become of this young man of twenty with a broken heart!' Life experiences can break some and make others. When the going gets tough the tough get going', but how many of us are tough?

Well as it happened life had something to offer Lolek. At the age of twenty-two he decided to become a Priest, after that he became a Bishop, after that again an Archbishop, then a Cardinal and finally a Pope. His name was Karol Wojytla who became Pope John Paul 11. His Mother called him 'Lolek' as her own pet name. This year 2020 (18th May) is the centenary of his birth, and 'Lolek' is now St. John Paul 11. So even if today is blue tomorrow is always new.

THE GALTYMORE

Brendan Shine has had a few interesting songs over his career. A most recent one that caught by attention is 'I met Her at the Galtymore'. That song would resonate with a lot of Irish People, so I did a little bit of research. First of all 'The Galtymore' was a Ballroom in Cricklewood, London. Maybe I was the only one who didn't know that. Whatever about the swinging 60's this place was swinging for more than one decade. It opened in 1952 and closed in 2008.

In between it was such an important meeting place for the Irish emigrants. Larry Cunningham could not believe his eyes when he saw the crowd who came to see him play at the Galtymore in 1967. He was actually a carpenter himself by trade, but they came to hear his singing voice on that occasion. Larry knocked the Beatles off top spot of the charts in 1966 with his 'Tribute to Jim Reeves'. Not bad for a carpenter!

Around the same time his song 'Lovely Leitrim' captivated all in Ireland, England and America. This song was written by a native Leitrim man who had emigrated to America in 1892, and often dreamed of his home County. Philip Fitzpatrick became a Policeman in New York, and was killed on duty there in 1947. His dreams of returning to see his home village of Aughavas at least one more time never materialised, but he has left us with his song 'Lovely Leitrim'.

'Big Tom doesn't Play here Anymore' went a song sung by Tom Allen, and I thought it a fantastic title. It summed up the feeling of a lot of people with the closure of Ballrooms in Ireland, and England. You can see the run-down Ballrooms all chained up in your minds eye, and in reality too. From being full of life and energy to abandonment and emptyness. So it's nice to see Brendan Shine reviving memories of earlier times. Many Emigrants left for England in the mid 1900's

I remember my next door neighbour, Mike Staunton, heading off with tears in his eyes. However, every cloud has a silver lining as he returned home some years later with a lovely bride, Mary from among the Wicklow Hills. Mike had met her at the Galtymore! Another neighbour, Padraig Staunton, found himself down in a trench in Birmingham laying cables. He came back too and became a Priest. A great experience for a Priest I would imagine! Did not the Irish build England and America, with the help of a few others of course.

And so, Big Tom does not play at the Galtymore anymore. Just as he does not play at the Royal Ballroom in Castlebar, at the Roseland in Moate, or the Cresent in Athlone. Donagal Man Johnny McCawley wrote Big Tom's hit 'Four Country Roads', and Larry's 'Among the Wicklow Hills'. All those songs meant so much to the Irish in England, with thoughts of their homeland in mind. Now Brendan Shine is keeping those nostalgic memories alive with 'I met her at the Galtymore',

I left old Ireland behind
No more my land to see
Tears have dried in my eyes
Thinking of Family.

I walked through briary brambles
As a child some nuts to gather
Then out to the boggy patch
To smell the colourful heather

Ah, they are days long ago
My journey is near its end
Now it's time for my bed
Angels tonight God may send.

Train *gone, memories* remain

TURNPIKE ROAD

The Child crawled across the Highway from her own house to the neighbour's house, her first signs of exploration. An extremely dangerous thing to do you might say. However, the highway was a grassy boreen, and it happened over a century ago. Years later a Bride, maybe the same baby, came across the boreen again to marry the across-the-road neighbour. One of the houses was my Mother's in Guesdian.

She told me that story, and it came down to her from her own Mother. Our Mothers told us many stories when we were young, but were we listening? The only danger on that highway might be a donkey and Cart; which could be dangerous too. That green grassy boreen was part of a thriving little village at the time. Many such Boreen's there were in Ireland, and families were for the most part self-sufficient.

They had the cow for milk, the hens, ducks, and turkeys for eggs. The field for potatoes, oats, wheat. The bog for turf and the donkey to pull the cart. Not forgetting the refreshing spring well. The sowing machine of the local Dress-maker can still be seen amongst the ruins of her old house there. A sight to take you back in time! Dresses are now made in bulk in far-off lands, maybe with cheap labour, and sold in our local Supermarkets. Time moves on and they tell us we have progressed, but we're rushing more than ever.

The modern roads help us to rush even more still, and the modern cars are 'happy' to oblige. There are twenty four hours in a day so rushing should be the exception rather than the rule. You can't hold back progress I suppose, but we must be headed in the right direction. Anyway there were no tolls on the far-away boreens, but I just read that the first tolls in Ireland came into existence in 1729. That's almost 300 years ago, and you might be thinking there were no roads then never mind tolls.

Obviously there were no cars then, but there were stage-coaches pulled by a horse. Gates were placed across the road which were called Turnpikes, so the horse moved on when the toll was paid. I thought road tolls were a modern-day thing, but it seems they go back quite awhile. There is still one of those roads in existence around Balbriggan. It is called Turnpike Road, and you can still drive on part of it. On other parts I can have a nice car-free Sunday walk. *Rambling in autumn days, through hedgerows of blackberries and hawthorns, soothes weary limbs and minds.*

On our modern day 'turnpike' roads you don't even have to stop to pay, just zoom by and the camera clicks your number. You still have to pay at some stage though, no free lunch, or drive in this case. Driving long distances takes its own toll, fatigue wise, and maybe we could start using the car less. At least we are heading towards the electric cars now, so less smoky exhausts. We travel down our own individual road, merging with others along the way. So many distractions can drive us down the wrong busy road, but we might be better off on the old turnpike road, or the tranquil grassy boreen.

Roads there are a' many, leading here and there
For you to find the right one, say a little prayer.

Some roads lead you north, others to east and west
Then you have the south one, search and seek the best

Roads may look attractive, but what's around the bend
The windy humble small one, may be best at roads end.

Photo: Thomas Reid

May the road rise to meet ye

LITTLE HOUSE

I would not have been given much to tears during my lifetime, but every time I watch 'Little House on the Prairie' I always end up crying. These would be tears of joy I suppose at the happy ending. If anybody walks in I cover my eyes, "so don't tell anybody I was crying now, do you hear". 'A little bit a tear let me down', sang Burl Ives. Most tears are shed in sorrow, upset, and tragedy. If we see somebody in tears we become upset, but they might be tears of healing.

I'm sure one of the main actors in 'Little House on the Prairie', Michael Landon, and his family had their moments of tears. He died in 1991 at the age of 54 from cancer. He had a saying: "If you want to do something do it now. There are only so many tomorrows". He had written a little poem for someone who died in the 'Little House' series: *Remember me with smiles and laughter, for that's the way I'll remember you all. If you remember me with tears, then don't remember me at all'.*

This poem was then read at his own funeral by his on-screen daughter Laura. A few tears for awhile are ok though I would imagine, and then remember the good times. Laura's own Father died when she was 11, so not only was Landon, Charles Ingalls, a Father to her in the TV series, he became a Father Figure to her also in real life. She said she felt completely secure in his company, and he told her that nothing is as important as Family.

He must have had some Irish blood because his Mother's maiden name was Peggy O'Neill. His Father's name was Eli Maurice Orowitz, Landon being a name Michael chose for his acting career. Laura's real name was Melissa Gilbert and her TV Mother Caroline, actress Karen Grassal, kept the Family ticking over nicely with her gentleness and wise words. Other family members were Mary, Albert and little Carrie; who was played by twins on alternate shows.

'Little house on the Prairie' was based on the series of 'Little House' books by Laura Ingalls Wilder. She was born in Walnut Grove, Minnesota in the late 1800's. In those good old times of the 1800's, but hard times, the old Priest in the series once sighed words to this effect: "It's hard to understand why God allows such suffering, but when it's over we see things differently". Ya, we do! In the final scene, with the exception of the Chapel and the Little House itself, the whole set, village in this case, was blown up. No turning back there!

The secret of the 'little house' is that it was a 'Home'. Bricks and mortar, or wood in this case, is only a shell. It needs the warmth of family to make it a home, and that's what the Little House on the Prairie was. Like a lot of other things we don't make films like that anymore. Maybe we have become too sophisticated, and the simplicity of olden times would not fit in with our modern tangled way of thought. I must say I like some of those artistically designed houses on telly, now turn them into a home! I'll go now, 'Little House' has just started.

ABBEY IN THE VALLEY

We often passed the Abbey in the Valley, Da and me, when I was a child. More often than not we missed it, as the roof is at the same level as the road. Missing it's history is a more difficult thing to do; 800 years of it. Yes, Ballintubber Abbey celebrates it's 8th centenary. It has been called 'The Abbey that Refused to Die', and sure enough it's now more alive than ever. I think another 800 years at least awaits it, if we are to view it in it's present condition.

Anyway Da and me had our own thoughts as we passed by in his van, travelling towards Drummin beside 'The Reek'. Up we'd go into the mountains to buy some calves and then sell them at Westport Fair. It was a day of Saturday freedom and adventure for me. Da passed away then and I grew up, I think, and moved away from home. But no matter how much we burn our bridges our roots are deep. I had to come back and look into the history of 'The Abbey in the Valley'.

Croagh Patrick, or 'The Reek' as we locals call it, looks down on the Abbey. It's another 800 years back since St Patrick prayed and fasted on this Holy Mountain, banishing the snakes along his path. Pilgrims walk from the Abbey to the 'Reek' today on Tochar Phadraig, St Patrick's Causeway, which was restored in 1987 by Fr Frank Fahey.

Ballintubber Abbey was founded in 1216 by the King of Connaught, Cathal Crovdearg O'Connor. In all those centuries there are no built-up areas around the Abbey, it remains in its tranquil setting surrounded by green fields The story of the Abbey goes like this: Before he was King, Cathal worked for a kind man in Ballintubber called Mr Sheridan. Later, as a reward for his kindness, the King promised to build a Chapel in place of the old one. Somehow the builders got it wrong and built the Chapel at another Ballintubber, in Co Roscommon.

When the King returned he found no new Chapel in Mayo, where had it gone to? After making inquiries he found that the Chapel had been built in the 'wrong' Ballintubber. Every cloud has a silver lining as they say, so the King said that he would build a Church seven times more magnificent, on the right site this time; hence Ballintubber Abbey today. So the motto is: don't stay discouraged after a mistake, just right the wrong by doing something better than the original plan.

Ballintubber means 'Townland of the Well' and St Patrick baptised pilgrims here in this Well while making his way to Croagh Patrick. Sometimes we locals don't appreciate the treasure on our doorstep. Far-away hills are green, but we must not forget to experience the local, maybe seeing it in a different light. We crave for far-away Holy Sites, which can be uplifting. However, Ballintubber Abbey, dedicated to the Holy Trinity, stands still, local, homely and blessed.

The Abbey stands calm in the mist,
defying the ravages of time.
Looks immovable in it's 800 years
Mankind's Faith keeps it so.

The 'Reek' stands tall in the distance
1600 years ago Patrick there prayed
Banishing the snakes along his Path
He stopped at the Abbey to pray.

God's house will stay as we pass on
Comforting its next generation
Reminding people what Life's about
This Abbey that refused to die.

THE ATLANTIC OCEAN

There's a little lake on Westport's doorstep, and on the doorstep of New York, called the Atlantic Ocean. If this Ocean could speak what stories it would have to tell! It was the scene of the Titanic disaster, and the Bermuda Triangle where planes and ships mysteriously disappeared. The misery of the coffin ships haunt many! On the other hand this water has brought many joyous people back to their homeland. So the Atlantic is a big part of Irish history; the watery part.

The Ocean is a place of storms rocking ships up and down. Then comes the calmness of the sea with tranquil views ahead. Under the Ocean then there is another world, oblivious to humanity most of the time, and us to it. The tiniest of fish inhabit this underwater world, as do the monstrous whales. The teethy sharks are there, and the friendly dolphins. We would advise the smiley crocodiles to experience the far out waters too.

We have 'The Wild Atlantic Way', stretching from Donegal to Cork in Ireland. Lots of stormy weather recently, and wilder it's getting it seems! The Atlantic is the second largest Ocean, after the Pacific, and covers twenty per cent of the 'Earth'. The deepest part of the Ocean is about 28,000 feet down, that would make it over five miles in depth if my calculations are correct. Icebergs are both above and below the water, but the bit we see is just the 'tip of the iceberg'.

The mysterious Island of Hy-Brazil is, or may not be, out there about 200 miles from the Irish coast. This 'beautiful' land is circular in shape with a river flowing through the centre. It's covered in mist most of the time, but appears every seven years. While it can be seen it is believed by some that it can not be reached. Amazingly Hy-Brazil appeared on old maps, so maybe the 'Isle of the Blest' is out there somewhere. It may be the same place as Oisin's 'Tir na Nog'.

It's amazing the amount of water in the world, but according to the Bible water came before dry land. God said, *"Let the waters below the sky be gathered together in one place and let dry land appear"* (Genesis 1:9) The Atlantic Ocean is a big swimming pool for us to have on our doorstep, but like a lot of amazing things we take it for granted; we just see the edge. Where I live now I have the smaller swimming pool of the Irish Sea.

Actually the shortest distance from Ireland to reach land across the Atlantic Ocean would be Newfoundland. This Island is called 'Talamh an Eisc' (Land of Fish) The word Atlantic, from Greek mythology, means 'Sea of Atlas'. The Atlas Mountains are in Morocco, so they may have their own 'Atlantic Way'. Ireland may be a kind of mini buffer for the Continent as the wind and rain reaches us first, and then loses its gale force. We must take the rough with the smooth. We have the advantage of a big sea on our doorstep, so whatever it brings we must take. Anyway, let's breathe in our wild Atlantic breeze.

On she roars to her destination
Cutting large waves to shreads
Storms are just a gentle breeze
To this ships majestic gliding

Sharks stare in jaw-drop awe
Whales flap their flappy fins
The sea world has not had
Such an out of sea experience

Ice-berg stands calm and still
Hiding its strength below
Bringing this ship to its ending
Before it has had its beginning

"Have you packed your laptop, ipad and telegram paper"

MY 'WIND'OW

Relaxing into an early morning coffee
What do I see through my window
Autumn trees swaying in the wind
A shower of leaves float off
> *But one leaf hangs on*
Invisible wind causing a commotion
Behind the trees I see another window
What's happening inside I wonder
Perhaps a storm in a coffee cup
> *Let those within look out*

My minds window sees further a-sea
Chopping waves overwhelm a boat
Wet-jacketed men seem in chaos
The boat is like a tossed match-box
> *A guiding hand leads them*

Northerly blizzards pushing men back
Typhons uprooting houses, twisting metal
Mountainous waves rocking Ocean Liners
Hurricanes rushing by in a hurry
> *Come gentle breeze*
Spring wheat blows in a green wavy flow
Turning colours in the summer sun
Golden now in the autumn breeze
Soon cut down to become a winter loaf
> *This moment I appreciate*
Back to my window and coffee gone
Peaceful here but it's time to move on
To the outside world, and face the storms
Or meet and greet in a gentle wind
> *Roll on tomorrow's window*

AFTER THE VIRUS

This chapter may be more for the people of the future, looking back, than for the people of the present. Sure go on and read it now anyway. In some way there is not a lot to write about because the World is in lockdown, or lockup, with a corona-virus. We are still breathing of course, so where there is breath there is hope. There may also be more happening than we think; in peoples inner lives more than the outer active lives.

If you are reading this chapter in 2040 you might say: 'those were strange times'. However even stranger times might have overtaken them by then. People sometimes speak of 20/20 vision, but now that the year 2020 is here I doubt that anybody could have had the vision of what is now unfolding. Corona-virus is not new as it includes a large family of viruses. Covid-19 is one of them and is new, as we all know by now. Scientists seem to have identified it in 2019, hence the name Covid-19.

Last year the only thing talked about in Europe was Brexit, meaning Britain's breakaway from the European Union. Then suddenly Covid19 arrived and put everything else in the shade. You may not believe me but it's true, I asked the butcher for two chicken-covids instead of chicken-kievs. The butcher shop was in uproar with laughter. Hearty laughter in a time of pain renews our spirits. There is now a vaccine but it has been rushed through, is it ok?

Whatever about Brexit separating the peoples of Europe this Covid-19 virus has really done that. We are now like the Japanese bowing instead of hand-shaking. Maybe we didn't appreciate the hand-shake when we had it, I hope we have it back. How many times are we told 'wash your hands', and 'don't forget your mask if you want to go to work'. Unless it's a family member we have to keep two metres apart. 'Be together by staying apart', they tell us. We must stay at home if we are over 70, I must tell them that 80 is the new 70!

Pandemic means a disease that is prevalent in a whole Country or World-wide. It is said that 50 million people died of the 'Spanish flu' in 1918. Writing about a Pandemic in the same year as it's happening might be unusual, We hope we have made progress in medicine and science since 1918. Have we made progress in our living habits though?   This too will be forgotten, but we hope us Humans will have learned something. We are fragile Beings, on a turbulent planet, moving through the vast ever-expanding Universe. We need a guiding hand or we spin out of control.

We all thought that Brexit was the most used word of 2019, but according to the dictionary 'Climate-strike' is down as the most used word for that year. It's kinda two words to me but that's what it says. Now of course Covid 19 has over-taken both. Things can change in a flash!. With no planes in the sky at the moment perhaps our air will be purer, and our climate improve however small it may be. Every cloud has a silver lining!

Young people are leading the way on climate action. The Swedish Teenager, Greta Toonburg, made an interesting statement, she said: "I don't know why people are listening to me now, but I must make the most of it". Strike while the 'planet' is hot! Climate change reminds me of the time I saw a neighbour walking across the 'hidden' lake in front of our house. It's deep I believe! He was on his way with a load of hay on his back for the cattle. I had never seen that before or since. It was one unique moment in time! That winter the ice was so think that he took a chance and made it. Happily for him there was no ice brexit, and covid was far from his thoughts.

Gateway to nature's tranquility

OH, CHRISTMAS TREE

It all started in Bethlehem 2000 years ago, the Christian era that is. Humble beginnings can sometimes have amazing endings, and it's not over yet. The stable that night was better than a palace because that's all Mary and Joseph had. When Jesus arrived, with the palm trees whistling in the wind, that's all they wanted. Jerico, forty kilometres away, is the City of the Palms. The 'Little Town of Bethlehem' is just down the road from the Holy City of Jerusalem.

Ironically while Christianity has spread all over the World the number of Christians in Bethlehem today has dwindled. In the last fifty years of the old Millennium, 1950 to 2000, the number has dropped from 85% to 40%. Muslins are now the majority in Bethlehem. Nazareth, where Jesus grew up, has 30% of Christians. It is the largest Arab city of Israel and has a population of 77 thousand, Muslims are also in the majority here. I'm sure carpentry is still carried on in Nazareth by all sides.

On this new years eve 2020/21 I have a candle lit here whose flame came all the way from Bethlehem. A candle was lit in Bethlehem and carried through the different countries of Asia and Europe by the Boy Scouts. Finally it arrived in Balbriggan Church, and many other places, from where we took our individual lights. What a lovely idea it is! *The light shone in the darkness, and the darkness could not over-come it'*.

Christmas is a time for coming together, but Christmas 2020 was a time for staying apart because of the Covid 19. There was even talk of cancelling Christmas, but Christmas can never be cancelled. Could you imagine Joseph saying to Mary "we'll have to cancel Christmas Mary", NO. In fairness, as they say now-a-days, it was only the large gatherings they intended to cancel. Anyway, there were only three people at the first Christmas. So maybe we might return to our roots with smaller less-indulgent Christmas gatherings.

'The Holly and the Ivy' is a Christmas carol. I feel a bit sorry for the ivy because it has got a bad name. It is inclined to take over when it starts to grow. However ivy is really very nice when it has just one simple layer. It should remember that 'less is more', no over indulgence! Holly is beautiful with or without berries. I recently learned that holly has no thorns on the top of its tree. The reason being, wait for it, cattle can't reach that high. It sprouts thorns on the bottom leaves to protect itself from the chewing animals. Maybe trees have feeling after all.

Holly in some places is a symbol of Christ's 'crown of thorns', the red berries for his blood, and the evergreen as Life after death. Finally I may be blowing out the lights for some people at Christmas, but I do not agree with Christmas Trees in Church. Some are even placed up beside the Altar where more important things are taking place. Let's keep the trees in the wood and fields. Bethlehem, meaning 'house of bread' in Hebrew, is also the city of David.

DEPARTURE LOUNGE

There is a joke going around amongst the older folk which says: "We are now in the departure lounge". Whilst it is a joke it's also true. No ticket or luggage needed, just a free trip to eternity. From a human point of view we seem to have a struggle to be born, and a struggle to die. We are nice and cosy in the womb, but we would not want to stay there forever, would we! In the same way this life is like another womb, and then we should be ready to move on again, so don't get too cosy!

You might imagine that the body would become stronger as we grow old. We have developed so much year after year, but still as we grow old the body gets weaker and weaker. So if the body is getting weaker then it must be the spirit that is getting stronger, or should be. The body is just a housing for the spirit, and it's up to us to develop the spirit through the sufferings of the body.

You would wonder why we need the body to rise at all on the last day, as we are left with the more interesting spirit anyway. The body seems to have given us so much trouble in life, but hopefully it has done its job. Our bodies have played their part, taken us through life, and hopefully matured us. Of course maybe we couldn't have individuality without the body. Anyway someone greater than I says the body will rise on the last day, so who am I to even question. God's ways are not always our ways.

Actually we may not even know we are in the Departure Lounge, never mind the flight. It's a journey many have taken and we too will take sooner or later. My first cousin Mary (Devaney) Neary has taken that journey as I write. As she died in the month of May, and on her 77th birthday, the first thought to enter my mind was 'the May Flower'. Like the flowers that bloom in May, Our Lady's month, Mary blossomed out whenever we met her, and that sent us away blooming as well. *Walking in the field of flowers, when this Life on Earth is through.Flowers that will never wither, in a Land that's always new.*

So we pass on and we leave behind the memories people have of us. Memories are interesting things because while people have died our memories of them are alive. When we do eventually pass away we hope those left behind erase any bad memories they have of us, and remember the good. Anyway we pray we are ready for take-off, when our turn comes. Come to think of it Eternity starts in this life, as 'life is changed not ended'.

While we are still on this earth let's make the most of it. Martin Luther King said: "The Person who has nothing in life worth dying for, is not fit to live". I can understand that! Another Martin I know said: "If we are doing what we are supposed to be doing we will be happy". Some People say that nobody ever came back to tell us what's on the other side. Well that's not exactly true because Jesus came back. Somebody asked 'Joseph of Arimathea' why he gave Jesus his grave when he died. Joseph replied: "He only needed it for the weekend".

Even the King upon the hill
will end up down below
With expectant waiting
under the winter snow

Back to the clay we came from
after our years on earth
How did we spend it I wonder
since the time of our birth

The quietness of the graveyard
those frenzy activities ceased
A rumbling through the headstones
let's come to the heavenly feast.

We move on

LIFE IS A MYSTERY

I met a couple of people who said Life is NOT a mystery, so perhaps they have developed more than me. Maybe the majority of people don't even think about it. You would imagine too that with age the mystery becomes less 'mysterious', but I don't think so. I presume that for God Life is not a mystery, but he is happy to live in the mystery with us. Hopefully all will be revealed when we reach the Promised Land.

My first chapter asks: 'what is Life all about', so this last chapter must be a continuation, or a conclusion, of the first. The mystery might be in the chapters in between. It has been said: 'the more we know, the more we know we don't know.' If we search for happiness we may not find it, but if we ignore happiness it sometimes comes and sits on our shoulder like a butterfly. Mystery is a bit like that, if you try to figure it out you can't, but if you let it be new insights come gently to your mind and inspire you.

It would be nice if this chapter brought some closure to the first chapter, but there are many chapters in life. The word closure is used quite often now, but it only comes when we close our eyes on our last day on earth. Closures before that only lasts a short time. Obviously we all have little closures in life to look forward to, and it's nice when it happens. However, I feel some of us make a decision not to live until we get closure. That creates a blockage!

Now I must not underestimate the pain some people are going through after being wronged. We all need time to heal, and time is a great healer. We need great patience to: 'let go and let God'. Some terrible things have happened to people and they went on to become successful and happy. We try not to close our lives waiting for closure. Where am I going with this chapter you may wonder, and so do I. It's the closing chapter so maybe that's why I'm on closure, and it's very close.

Anyway back to the beautiful mystery of mystery. The thing we do most often in life we rarely think about. 'Breathing' is that thing and it seems to be so automatic. Now the 'ticking of the heart' might be a good challenger, as that happens quite often too. I suppose they go hand in hand, but which started first I will have to think about. Perhaps the heart starts first, as the Mother probably breathes for the baby before birth. I think I'll leave all that to the medics.

What can we really say about mystery except: 'it's a mystery.' Life consists of the little happenings of life which lead to bigger things. The past is gone and the future is coming, but someone said: 'now' is a gift and that's why it's called the present. Scientists will keep on discovering, but the ever expanding Universe will always be beyond their grasp in this life. Most times in our everyday activities we forget about any mystery. Then when our quite times come along this great question of Life comes to the fore. Closed for now!

Troubles, worries and pain
return again and again
Dark clouds around, sadness abounds
Life's a mystery

Images of what might have been
dreams of what may begin
The past's out of sight, the future looks bright
Life's a mystery

We walk in hope in the mystery
through the deep dark clouds towards eternity
We walk hand in hand till the gates we see
Of the Promised Land, beyond the mystery.

Meditating the Mystery

OTHER BOOKS by THIS AUTHOR

. . . .

THE CRANE

ARE THE DAFFODILS UP

CROSSROADS ACROSS TIMES

IMAGINE THAT: (This book is a combination of the best stories from the above three.)

tomhany@yahoo.co.uk

087 7737729

Tom Heneghan